The Eight Plays of Christmas

A Series of Radio Dramas

Julio Martinez

authorHOUSE

AuthorHouse™
1663 Liberty Drive
Bloomington, IN 47403
www.authorhouse.com
Phone: 1 (800) 839-8640

© 2018 Julio Martinez. All rights reserved.

No part of this book may be reproduced, stored in a retrieval system, or transmitted by any means without the written permission of the author.

The following eight works were originally broadcast over KPFK, Pacifica Radio for the Greater Los Angeles Area, and distributed nationally over the Pacific Radio Network. Two of the works, Keeping Christmas Well and A Christmas Eve Truce, were also broadcast over the BBC in Great Britain on Christmas Eve 2012 and 13. The play can be performed as staged readings or as theatrical productions.

Published by AuthorHouse 04/10/2018

ISBN: 978-1-5462-3691-7 (sc)
ISBN: 978-1-5462-3735-8 (e)

Library of Congress Control Number: 2018904484

Print information available on the last page.

Any people depicted in stock imagery provided by Getty Images are models, and such images are being used for illustrative purposes only. Certain stock imagery © Getty Images.

This book is printed on acid-free paper.

Because of the dynamic nature of the Internet, any web addresses or links contained in this book may have changed since publication and may no longer be valid. The views expressed in this work are solely those of the author and do not necessarily reflect the views of the publisher, and the publisher hereby disclaims any responsibility for them.

CONTENTS

The Gift Of The Magi 1
    (Adapted from the short story by O. Henry)

The Nutcracker's Journey 12
    (the story of the beloved Christmas ballet)

To All A Good Night 31
    (The Story of Santa Claus)

Keeping Christmas Well 56
    (The Journey to Dickens' "A Christmas Carol")

The Christmas Eve Truce 78
    (Christmas Eve on the Western Front, 1914)

All Is Calm, All Is Bright 92
    (The Story of "Silent Night")

One Horse Open Sleigh 110
    (The Story of "Jingle Bells")

Christmas In Tinseltown 136
    (The Story of "White Christmas")

THE GIFT OF THE MAGI

(ADAPTED FROM THE SHORT STORY BY O. HENRY)

By Julio Martinez

The Players

O Henry……………....middle aged author
Della……………..……wife, age 20
Jim………………....…..husband, age 2
Madame……………….middle aged hair merchant

CHRISTMAS MUSIC SEGUEING INTO SOUNDS OF A NOISY TAVERN

O HENRY

Thank you so much for the libation, sir. And yes, my name is William Sydney Porter, I guess better known by my alias, O. Henry. Any man who spent three years confinement in a state penitentiary like I have, should possess an alias. And you have caught me in a jolly mood this Christmas Eve 1905. I have just finished another story. Actually, I seem to write all my stories at this very table here at Pete's Tavern, the best watering hole on Irving Place. Set the drinks and yourself down and I will happily relate this tale of two poor silly young people who discover the true spirit of what this day is all about. As most dilemmas in this life, this story concerns money, more accurately, the lack of it.

CHRISMAS MUSIC SWELLS AND DIMINISHES

DELLA
One dollar and eighty-seven cents. That's all? And sixty cents of it is in pennies. Ten, twenty, thirty-five, forty-five, fifty, seventy-five, one dollar. **(DELLA CONTINUES COUNTING SOTTO VOCE WHILE THE NARRATOR CONTINUES)**

O HENRY
Pennies saved one and two at a time by bulldozing the grocer and the vegetable man and the butcher until her cheeks burned with the silent imputation of parsimony that such close dealing implied. Three times Della counted it.

DELLA
One dollar and eighty-seven cents. And tomorrow is Christmas. (SOBBING)
It's hopeless. What can I do?

O HENRY
There was clearly nothing to do but flop down on the shabby little couch and howl. So Della did it. Which instigates the moral reflection that life is made up of sobs, sniffles, and smiles, with sniffles predominating.

DELLA
(SNIFFLING) I can't face Christmas day without a present for Jim. What kind of wife am I?

O HENRY
While the mistress of the home is gradually subsiding from the first stage to the second, take a look at the home. A well-scrubbed but

meager furnished flat at $8 per week. In the vestibule below is a letter-box into which no letter would go, and an electric button from which no mortal finger could coax a ring. Also appertaining thereunto was a card bearing the name "Mr. James Dillingham Young." The "Dillingham" had been flung to the breeze during a former period of prosperity when its possessor was being paid $30 per week. Now, in the midst of more meager times, the income has shrunk to $20. Della's self-critical husband often stared at the card and scoffed.

JIM

A man who can't earn more than $20 a week doesn't deserve a full middle name on his letter box. Della, I am going to change it to just "James D."

O HENRY

But whenever Mr. James Dillingham Young came home and reached his flat above he was called "Jim" and greatly hugged by Mrs. James Dillingham Young, already introduced to you as Della. Which is all very good. But did not solve the problem currently at hand.

DELLA

Crying is not going to solve anything. I have to pull myself together. (SHE BLOWS HER NOSE) Where's my mirror? Oh, I am such a mess. Let's just figure this out. Tomorrow will be Christmas Day, and I have only $1.87 with which to buy Jim a present. Oh, it is so hopeless.

O HENRY

Della had been saving every penny she could for months, with this result. Twenty dollars a week doesn't go far. Expenses had been greater than she had calculated. They always are. Only $1.87 to buy a present for Jim. Her Jim. Many a happy hour she had spent planning for something nice for him.

DELLA

Something fine and rare and sterling--something just a little bit near to being worthy of the honor of being owned by my Jim.

O HENRY

Della was staring out the window, reflecting on how much she loved this man who was her husband. Suddenly she whirled from the window and quickly lifted up her small mirror and stared intently at her own reflection. Her eyes were shining brilliantly, but her face lost its color as a plan started to formulate as she continued to gaze at her own countenance.

DELLA

My hair!

O HENRY

Rapidly she pulled down her hair and let it fall to its full length. Now, there were two possessions of the James Dillingham Youngs in which they both took a mighty pride. One was Jim's gold watch that had been his father's and his grandfather's. The other was Della's hair. Had the queen of Sheba lived in the flat across the airshaft, Della would have let her hair hang out the window some day to dry just to depreciate Her Majesty's jewels and gifts. Had King Solomon been the janitor, with all his treasures piled up in the basement, Jim would have pulled out his watch every time he passed, just to see him pluck at his beard from envy.

DELLA

(REFLECTIVELY) Jim so dearly loves his watch….and my hair grows so quickly.

O HENRY

So now Della's beautiful hair fell about her rippling and shining like a cascade of brown waters. It reached below her knee and made itself almost a garment for her. And then she did it up again nervously and quickly. Once she faltered for a minute and stood still while a tear or two splashed on the worn red carpet. On went her old brown jacket; on went her old brown hat. With a whirl of skirts and with the brilliant sparkle still in her eyes, she fluttered out the door and down the stairs to the street. She practically ran passed the many shop signs that proclaimed the wares being sold along Broadway.

SOUNDS OF THE STREET

DELLA
Where is it? I know I have seen it a hundred times. Where is that sign? Oh, there it is: "Mne. Sofronie. Hair Goods of All Kinds."

O HENRY
One flight up Della ran, and collected herself, panting. Madame was conspicuous by her presence…large, too white, chilly, hardly looking the "Sofronie." Sitting in front of her open doorway, this rotund woman cast a coolly calculating glance at Della as the young woman paused to regain her composure.

MADAME
You have business with me? Do not waste my time.

DELLA
Will you buy my hair?

MADAME
That is an interesting question. I buy hair. But not everyone's hair deserves to be bought. Come in. Take yer hat off and let's have a sight at the looks of it.

O HENRY
As if she were facing an executioner, Della slowly took off her hat and took the pins out of her hair. Down rippled the brown cascade. As her hair descended to its full length, Della did not notice Madame's

eyes quickly widen as her lips let out a silent gasp at the full glory that shone before her.

MADAME
(CAUTIOUSLY) You wish to sell this hair?

DELLA
Yes…if you can give me a good price.

O HENRY
At the mention of money, Madame's face took on an icy, noncommittal visage. She lifted the mass of hair with a practiced hand, allowing the tresses to flow luxuriously through her aged fingers.

MADAME
I give you twenty dollars. In better times, perhaps I could offer more but…

DELLA
Yes. Give it to me quick.

MADAME
You are in a hurry but you must sit down and be patient as I use the scissors. I am an expert and will not be rushed.

DELLA
Yes, I will be patient but I do have so much to do. This is Christmas Eve.

MUSIC SWELLS AND THEN DIMINISHES

O HENRY
The twenty dollars well protected in her purse, Della flew through the next two hours on rosy wings. Forget the hashed metaphor. She ransacked the stores for Jim's present. She found it at last.

DELLA
This is it. It surely was made for Jim and no one else. There was nothing like this in any of the stores and I must have turned all of them inside out.

O HENRY
In her trembling hands, Della held a platinum fob chain, simple and chaste in design, properly proclaiming its value by substance alone and not by meretricious ornamentation…As all good things should do. It was even worthy of The Watch. As soon as she saw it she knew that it must be Jim's. It was like him. The written description,

"Quietness and value," applied to both. Twenty-one dollars they took from her for it, and she hurried home with the 87 cents.

DELLA
With this chain on his watch Jim might be properly anxious about the time in any company. My poor Jim. Grand as the watch is, I have seen him sometimes look at it on the sly on account of the old leather strap that he uses in place of a chain.

O HENRY
When Della reached home her intoxication gave way a little to prudence and reason. She got out her curling irons and lighted the gas and went to work repairing the ravages made by generosity added to love. Which is always a tremendous task, dear friend--a mammoth task. Within forty minutes her head was covered with tiny, close-lying curls that made her look wonderfully like a truant schoolboy. She looked at her reflection in the mirror long, carefully, and critically.

DELLA
If Jim doesn't kill me before he takes a second look at me, he'll say I look like a Coney Island chorus girl. But what could I do? Oh! What

could I do with a dollar and eighty- seven cents? Enough of this. It's done. I must start supper.

O HENRY

At 7 o'clock the coffee was made and the frying-pan was on the back of the stove hot and ready to cook the chops. Jim was never late. Della doubled the fob chain in her hand and sat on the corner of the table near the door that he always entered. Then she heard his step on the stair away down on the first flight, and she turned white for just a moment. She had a habit for saying little silent prayer about the simplest everyday things, and now she whispered:

DELLA

Please God, make him think I am still pretty.

O HENRY

The door opened and Jim stepped in and closed it. In the few seconds it took before Jim would look at her, Della took stock of the man she loved so dearly.

DELLA

He looks so thin and so very serious. Poor fellow, he is only twenty-two--and to be burdened with a family! He needs a new overcoat and he is without gloves.

O HENRY

Jim stopped inside the door, as immovable as a setter at the scent of quail. His eyes were fixed upon Della, and there was no expression in them that she could not read, and it terrified her. It was not anger, nor surprise, nor disapproval, nor horror, nor any of the sentiments that she had been prepared for. He simply stared at her fixedly with that peculiar expression on his face. Della wriggled off the table and went for him.

The Eight Plays of Christmas

DELLA

Jim, darling, don't look at me that way. I had my hair cut off and sold it because I couldn't have lived through Christmas without giving you a present. It'll grow out again. You won't mind, will you? I just had to do it. My hair grows awfully fast. Say 'Merry Christmas!' Jim, and let's be happy. You don't know what a nice-- what a beautiful, nice gift I've got for you."

JIM

(LABORIOUSLY) You've cut off your hair?

DELLA

Cut it off and sold it. Don't you like me just as well, anyhow? I'm me without my hair, ain't I?"

JIM

(CATATONICALLY LOOKING ABOUT) You say your hair is gone?

DELLA

You needn't look for it, Jim. It's sold, I tell you--sold and gone, too. It's Christmas Eve, boy. Be good to me, for it went for you. (TAKING A DIFFERENT TACT) Maybe the hairs of my head were numbered, but nobody could ever count my love for you. Shall I put the chops on, Jim?

O HENRY

Out of his trance, Jim seemed quickly to wake. He enfolded his Della. For many seconds he held her tightly. He then slowly held her away from him. Jim drew a package from his overcoat pocket and threw it upon the table.

JIM

Dell, don't make any mistake about me. I don't think there's anything in the way of a haircut or a shave or a shampoo that could make me like my girl any less. But if you'll unwrap that package you may see why you had me going a while at first.

DELLA

(ECSTATICALLY) For me? Oh Jim, what can this be? This is such a nice box. Oh Jim its….its (MILDLY HORRIFIED Oh no. What have I done? Oh Jim, what have I done? (SOBS)

JIM

Dell, my dear Dell. Come here, Please.

O HENRY

Jim realized the current revelation would necessitate the immediate employment of all the comforting powers of the lord of the flat. For in the box lay The Combs--the set of combs, side and back, that Della had worshipped long in a Broadway window. Beautiful combs, pure tortoise shell, with jewelled rims--just the shade to wear in the beautiful vanished hair. They were expensive combs, she knew, and her heart had simply craved and yearned over them without the least hope of possession. And now, they were hers, but the tresses that should have adorned the coveted adornments were gone. But she hugged them to her bosom, and at length she was able to look up with dim eyes and a smile.

DELLA

My hair grows so fast, Jim! Oh, oh! Jim, you haven't seen your beautiful present.

O HENRY

She held it out to him eagerly upon her open palm. The dull precious metal seemed to flash with a reflection of her bright and ardent spirit.

DELLA

Isn't it a dandy, Jim? I hunted all over town to find it. You'll have to look at the time a hundred times a day now. Give me your watch. I want to see how it looks on it.

O HENRY
Instead of obeying, Jim tumbled down on the couch and put his hands under the back of his head and smiled.

JIM
Dell, let's put our Christmas presents away and keep 'em a while. They're too nice to use just at present. Dell…I pawned the watch to get the money to buy your combs. And now suppose you put the chops on. Merry Christmas, Dell.

DELLA
Merry Christmas, Jim. **BOTH JIM AND DELLA BEGIN A SIMPLE CHUCKLE THAT GROWS AND SOON FILLS THEIR SMALL HOME WITH LAUGHTER.**

O HENRY
The magi, as you know, were wise men--wonderfully wise men--who brought gifts to the Babe in the manger. They invented the art of giving Christmas presents. Being wise, their gifts were no doubt wise ones. And here I have lamely related to you the uneventful chronicle of two foolish children in a flat who most unwisely sacrificed for each other the greatest treasures of their house. But in a last word to the wise of these days, let it be said that of all who give gifts these two were the wisest. <u>They</u> are the magi.

CHRISTMAS MUSIC SWELLS.

The End

THE NUTCRACKER'S JOURNEY

A Radio Play
Written By Julio Martinez

The Cast

Narrrator (any age)
E.T.A. Hoffmann (writer, late 30s)
Maria Hoffmann (Hoffman's wife, early 30s)
Monsieur Valentin (publisher, early 30s)
Madame Valentin (Valentin's wife, early30s)
Michelle Valentin (13-year-old)
Andre Valentin (11-year-old)
Alexandre Dumas (author, early 40s)
Pyotr Ilyich Tchaikovsky (composer, early 50s
Ivan Vsevolozhsky (Director, Imperial Theatres, 60s)
Mily Balakirev (composer, 40s)
William Christensen (Founder, San Francisco Ballet, early 40s)
Margaret (Business Manager, San Francisco Ballet, 50s)

THEME FROM THE NUTCRACKER (15 SECONDS) THEN LOWERED TO UNDERSCORE THE NARRATOR

NARRATOR

Ernest Theodor Wilhelm Hoffmann, better known by his penname, E.T.A. Hoffman, was born in Köningsberg, Prussia on January 24, 1776.

In his youth, he easily mastered academics and the arts, but was principally drawn toward music, having developed an obsession for Wolfgang Amadeus Mozart.

MOZART'S OVERTURE TO 'THE MARRIAGE OF FIGARO (15 SECONDS)

HOFFMAN
"Music is the most romantic of all the arts, one might almost say, the only genuinely romantic art, for its own sole subject is the infinite."

NARRATOR
But the muse-bitten young man was also practical.
He entered the University of Köningsberg, where he studied law. In 1802 he married Maria Thekla Michaelina Rorer-Tracinska and for most of his life, Hoffman worked as a Prussian law officer, all the while hoping to foster a cultural identity as a composer and conductor.
But by 1814, despite some modest success, Hoffmann recognized he would never be a great composer.
He decided to explore an alternate form of artistic expression.

MARIA
Herr Hoffmann, it is late.
You have to be in court very early in the morning.

HOFFMANN
I have to finish this opening chapter.
Then I'll come to bed, Maria.

MARIA

Opening chapter? What about the Cantata you were working on?

HOFFMANN

Maria, my compositions are little more than fodder for church services.
I believe I can say more with the written word.

MARIA

What is it you wish to say?

HOFFMANN

I want to accomplish with words what Ludwig says with his music.

MARIA

Ludwig? Von Beethoven?
That unwashed malcontent who wanders the streets babbling to himself?
He stinks.

HOFFMANN

Forget his hygiene.
Beethoven's music speaks unrelenting truth.
It sets in motion the lever of fear, of awe, of horror, of suffering, and awakens that infinite longing which I believe is the primal force of our humanity.

MARIA

My goodness, Herr Hoffmann, what is it you are writing?

HOFFMANN

A children's book.

MARIA

A Children's book? What is it called?

HOFFMANN

The Nutcracker. It is a fantasy about a maiden who strives to help a young man who has been cursed, and in doing so, puts her own life in danger.

MARIA

What curse?

HOFFMAN

He has been turned into a nutcracker.

MARIA

Oh. And what's her danger?

HOFFMAN

I don't know yet.
But it will be deeply psychological.
I mean to probe the inner sanctum of a child's psyche and unleash the emotional demons that reside within.

MARIA

My husband, I do not believe parents want their children's demons unleashed.
They want their children well behaved.

HOFFMANN

And that is just what is wrong with German society today.
It is relentlessly ridged, strict and conformist.
Children are stifled and kept in emotional check, expected to act like mini adults.
Freedom of a child's spirit can only be obtained by liberating the imagination.

MARIA

Well, Herr Hoffmann, I hope you are able to release your imagination with opening arguments in court tomorrow. The law is your profession, and maintaining this household is mine.

I am going to bed.

MARIA SCREAMS

Eeeeek!

HOFFMANN

Maria! What's wrong?

MARIA

A mouse just ran by my feet and into the kitchen... a horrible dirty mouse.

HOFFMANN

Maria, I will deal with the mouse in the morning. Go up to bed.

MARIA

You will get rid of it?

MARIA EXITS. HOFFMANN CALLS AFTER HER.

HOFFMANN

Maria, I know you loathe mice.
as do most people, but they really are harmless.
Wait....Mice! Where is my title page?

RUSTLES THROUGH PAPERS

Here now.

The Nutcracker. Hmm.
The Nutcracker...and the Mouse King." Yes, that's it.

THEME FROM *ODE TO JOY*

NARRATOR
Despite Frau Hoffmann's doubts and a smattering of critical reservations about the darkness of its themes, *The Nutcracker and the Mouse King*, was generally well-received, as well as Herr Hoffmann's subsequent prose.
At the time of his death in 1826, E.T.A. Hoffmann was eulogized as one of the guiding lights of Europe's burgeoning 19th Century Romantic movement.
In fact, he was the central figure in Jacques Offenbach's 1850s opera, *The Tales of Hoffmann*.
But in 1844, in the Paris offices of Chapman and Hall Publishers, there was one dissenting voice that would have a profound effect on the future of Hoffmann's supposed children's book.

MADAME VALENTIN
OFF MIKE Monsieur Valentin, Monsieur Valentin, I must speak with you this minute And we refuse to wait in your outer offices.
Come with me children.

MICHELLE & ANDRE
Oui, Mama.

ANDRE
OFF MIKE Quit pushing

MICHELLE
Stop hitting me.

Julio Martinez

ON MIKE   **MADAME VALENTIN**
Children! Behave.
Monsieur Valentin!

VALENTIN
Madam Valentin.
I am in a meeting?

MADAME VALENTIN
I beg your pardon.
I did not know you had company.
We will wait in the outer lobby.
But you and I must speak.

ALEXANDRE DUMAS
No, no. Please stay. Monsieur Valentin and I have concluded our negotiations, quite favorably for me, I must say.
Sir, please introduce me to this lovely, impassioned woman and her handsome children.

VALENTIN
Sir, this is no impassioned woman;
this is my wife, Madame Valentin and our, children Michelle and Andre.
Madame, may I have the honor of introducing my new client, Monsieur Alexandre Dumas.

ANDRE
Oh. You wrote *The Fencing Master*.
Great fighting.

MICHELLE
I read it too. It was a wonderful adventure story.

The Eight Plays of Christmas

MADAME VALENTIN
I as well. It is an honor, sir.
You are a truly gifted writer

DUMAS
Monsieur Valentin. May I congratulate you on the astute literary scholars residing in your own household.

VALENTIN
Well, Madame, children.
You will be happy to know that Chapman and Hall has negotiated to publish Monsieur Dumas' next novel, *The Count of Monte Christo*.
I will be his official representative in Paris.

MADAME VALENTIN
I am delighted my husband has made such a wise decision, unlike the catastrophe he had me read this morning.

VALENTIN
Madame!

MADAME SLAMS A BOOK ON THE TABLE

MADAME
Tell me you are not going to publish this horrible book.

VALENTIN
The Nutcracker and the Mouse King by E, T.A. Hoffmann?
Yes. We are handling the French and English translations.
It's a children's book.
That is why I had you read it.

MADAME

Children? This is not meant for children.
It was written for guillotine operators.
It is brutal. Broken bones and teeth, disfigurement, children dying.

VALENTIN

But Madame…

MADAME

I don't care if they are mouse children.
They are still children. And this Hoffman had the nerve to set it at Christmastime.

MICHELLE

It was pretty scary.

ANDRE

I liked it.

VALENTIN

Madame, in Germany, this book is a classic.

MADAME

I wager it is…in Germany.
This is France. Our children need to be enlightened, not terrified.

DUMAS

I have read the book in the original German.
There are some very dark elements to it, but there are also some deeply captivating flights of fancy. It has merit.
It just needs to be lightened up somewhat.

MICHELLE

Actually, the end part where the Nutcracker turns back into a prince and marries the maiden...
That was beautiful.

ANDRE

I liked the killing.

VALENTIN

Monsieur Dumas, I have an idea.
At best, Hoffmann's text is a novelette.
Would you be interested in writing your own version of the story?
Heighten the fanciful sections and make less obvious Hoffmann's Teutonic musings.
It would be one famous writer, honoring another famous writer.

DUMAS

I am not that famous.

VALENTIN

Believe me, Monsieur Alexandre Dumas, once *The Count of Monte Christo* is published, you will be.

DUMAS

Sounds like great fun. I'll do it.
But to differentiate between the two versions, I will call mine, *The Nutcracker's Tale*.

MADAME

Viva la France!

Julio Martinez

OFFENBACH OVERTURE TO 'THE TALES OF HOFFMAN' (20 SECONDS)

NARRATOR

The Nutcracker and the Mouse King and *The Nutcracker's Tale* were both in circulation throughout the 19th century, often purchased as companion works. Hoffman's version was considered much more philosophically probing; but Dumas's revision was praised for its magic-laden storytelling.

In the summer of 1891, it was the latter version that was being scrutinized by Ivan Vsevolozhsky, the director of the Imperial Theatres of Moscow, much to the dismay of Russia's foremost composer, 51-year old Pyotr Ilyich Tchaikovsky.

TCHAIKOVSKY

Ivan, I am not going to compose another fairy tale ballet. I already did *Sleeping Beauty*. That's enough.

VSEVOLOZHSKY

And *Sleeping Beauty* is one of the most popular ballets ever performed by the Imperial Ballet.
Please read the book. It will inspire you.

TCHAIKOVSKY

I don't want to be inspired to compose a ballet based on some fanciful children's book.
I have been invited to conduct in Budapest and in Berlin.
I have discovered I actually like conducting.
That inspires me.

VSEVOLOZHSKY

Are you not also inspired by the commissions you receive from the Imperial Theatre?

TCHAIKOVSKY
Perhaps. What did you have in mind?

VSEVOLOZHSKY
We are prepared to offer you the largest commission the Imperial Theatre has ever allocated for a ballet. *Sleeping Beauty* fills the theatre whenever it is performed. I want another ballet that puts bottoms in seats and makes lots of money.

TCHAIKOVSKY
That's it? You want....a seat filler.

VSEVOLOZHSKY
I do indeed.

TCHAIKOVSKY'S 1812 OVERTURE (10 SECONDS)

NARRATOR
The reluctant composer retreated to his apartment with Alexandre Dumas' tome in hand.
But it was with an air of mischief that Tchaikovsky enjoyed his coffee the next morning with fellow composer, Mily Balakirev.

TCHAIKOVSKY
Mily, Vsevolozhsky wants a theatre full of behinds, no matter what the music sounds like.
And I'm going to give it to him.

BALAKIREV
And just how do you propose to do that?

TCHAIKOVSKY

By making it sweeter than the six lumps of sugar you put in your coffee every morning.

Mily, I promise you I am going to give Ivan a ballet with so many syrupy melodic sweeps, our esteemed Director will be inflicted with gout.

BALAKIREV

Since you're approaching this commission with your tongue planted firmly in your cheek, would you like to make the task a bit more interesting?

TCHAIKOVSKY

How interesting?

BALAKIREV

A wager. I bet you 100 rubles that you cannot write a major theme for this ballet, based only on the notes of the diatonic scake in sequence, your basic do, re, me, fa, sol, la, ti, do.

TCHAIKOVSKY

Does it matter whether the notes are in ascending or descending order?

Perhaps, do, ti, la, sol, fa, me, re, do?

BALAKIREV

That is purely up to you. You're the composer.

OPENING 16 BARS OF TCHAIKOVSKY PIANO CONCERTO #1

NARRATOR

The composer went about his task and Vsevolozhsky scheduled *The Nutcracker Ballet* to make its debut

The Eight Plays of Christmas

in December 1892 at the Imperial Theatre in St. Petersburg.

Knowing that his friend was disdaining the compositional task set before him, Mily Balakirev was surpised when Tchaikovsky invited him in March of that year to an orchestral rehearsal of the work at the St. Petersburg Conservatory, where they both served on the faculty.

SOUND OF INSTRUMENTS TUNING UP

BALAKIREV

Well sir, ready so soon? Knowing how you feel, I thought you would drag this score out to the bitter end.

TCHAIKOVSKY

The ballet score is not completely ready.

But I have made a selection of eight themes from the ballet, forming a *Nutcracker Suite*. I intend to perform a concert of the later this month for the St. Petersburg Musical Society.

BALAKIREV

You certainly seem much more enthusiastic than you were last year.

TCHAIKOVSKY

Mily, it is surprising to me as well.

I am daily becoming more and more attuned to my task.

I particularly wanted you to hear one section of the work.

ADDRESSING THE ORCHESTRA

Gentleman, would you please turn to the Grand Adagio…and

Julio Martinez

THE OPENING SECTION OF *THE GRAND ADAGIO* FROM THE *GRAND PAS DE DEUX FROM THE* SECOND ACT OF THE BALLET

BALAKIREV
(LISTENING TO THE MUSIC, WHOSE THEME CLEARLY OUTLINES A DESCENDING DIATONIC SCALE)
Ilyitch, you rascal. You have won.

NARRATOR
At the conclusion of the Grand Adagio, Balakirev gladly handed the 100 rubles he had wagered, for Tchaikovsky had indeed won the bet.
The Nutcracker ballet premiered December 18.
The children's roles, unlike many later productions, were performed by real children, students of the Imperial Ballet School of St. Petersburg.
Alas, unlike the spectaculor debut of *Sleeping Beauty* three years earlier, the first performance of *The Nutcracker* was not deemed a success; but over the years it did grow in popularity.

DANCE OF THE SUGAR PLUM FAERIES (20 SECONDS)

NARRATOR (CONT'D)
The first complete performance outside Russia took place in England in 1934.
It took a little longer to reach the United States.
The matter of World War II got in the way.
In fact, on December 1, 1944, William Christensen, the Artistic Director of the San Francisco Ballet, wasn't sure his company would survive the war.

WILLIAM CHRISTENSEN
What do you mean the company is bankrupt?

The Eight Plays of Christmas

MARGARET

Mr. Christensen, we have no money in the bank and we pretty much owe every vendor in San Francisco and beyond. That is what I mean by bankrupt.

CHRISTENSEN

But we have subscribers who paid for a whole season. Where did that money go?

MARGARET

Oh let me see. It went for the costumes and salaries for *Petrushka*. It went for costumes and salaries for *Swan Lake*.
It went for...

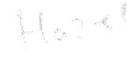

CHRISTENSEN

All right, I get it.

MARGARET

Mr. Christensen...William, the problem isn't with the subscribers. We are not getting any walkup sales.
I think with the war on, the average citizen is more likely to want to see Benny Goodman at the Pavillion than a ballet at the Opera House.

CHRISTENSEN

So, you are telling me we are dead?
You are saying we can't mount a final production this year?

MARGARET

I am your business manager, not a magician.
You don't need another ballet, you need an event that will draw people in off the street. You need magic.

27

CHRISTENSEN

Magic. How do I do that? I can't buy or rent costumes.
I can't pay salaries.

MARGARET

Actually, there is a reserve fund that will allow the company two weeks of salaries, but no costumes. Whatever you do will have to be done with what we have in storage.

CHRISTENSEN

What do we have?

MARGARET

Swan Lake, *Petrushka*, that's about it.
Oh, the ballet school performed *March of the Tin Soldiers* this summer and, oh yes, the *Country Mouse and the City Mouse*.
It was quite charming. All those little mice dancing about.

CHRISTENSEN

Whoa, whoa. We have tin soldier and mouse costumes? How many?

MARGARET

William, it's a ballet school.
Every mother wants to see her little Nijinsky or Pavlova on stage.
We have lots of costumes.

CHRISTENSEN

What sizes?

MARGARET

Children come in all sizes.
The costumes are in all sizes.

The Eight Plays of Christmas

CHRISTENSEN

The costumes, the costumes.
Swans can become sugar plumb faeries;
the Petrusha villagers are the people at the party.
Tin soldiers can become Nutcracker soldiers;
and we have a mouse army. We can do it.

MARGARET

We can do what?

CHRISTENSEN

The American premiere of Tchaikovsky's greatest stagework, *The Nutcracker Ballet.*
The Ballet Russe did an abridged version of it in New York four years ago.
But the full ballet has never been performed in the United States.

MARGARET

I didn't know that was his greatest stagework.

CHRISTENSEN

It is now. The ballet takes place on Christmas Eve.
I want to make a press announcement that The San Francisco Ballet is going to premiere *The Nutcracker Ballet* on December 24.
We'll make it an annual event, the Company's holiday gift to the citizens of San Francisco.

MARGARET

They still have to buy tickets.

CHRISTENSEN

Of course they have to pay for the tickets.
The "gift" is the magnificence of our production.

I saw the Ballet Russe's version.
Tchaikovsky's music is a miracle.
I optioned the complete ballet four years ago.
but was going to wait until after the war to produce it.
We're not waiting.
And our production will be an annual holiday tradition
for as long as there is a San Francisco Ballet.

MUSIC SWELLS AND PROVIDES AN UNDERCURRENT FOR THE NARRATION

NARRATOR

Indeed. *The Nutcracker* is to this day the annual highlight of the San Francisco Ballet Season.
Within ten years of its 1944 debut, companies around the world began to emulate San Francisco's success, choreographed by such notables as George Balanchine, Rudolf Nureyev and Mikhail Baryshnikov.
Happy Holidays to all.

MUSIC SWELLS

The End

TO ALL A GOOD NIGHT

(THE STORY OF SANTA CLAUS)

A Radio Play
Written By Julio Martinez

Cast

Santa Claus (mid 50s)
Mrs. Claus (mid 50s)
Thaddeus (mid 30s)
Bishop Nicholas of Smyrna (60s)
Governor John Winthrop (mid 30s)
Washington Irving (early 30s)
Elizabeth Pintard (late 20s)
John Pintard (late 20s)
Louise Pintard (12 years old)
Virginia O'Hanlan (8 years old)
Francis P. Church (early 40s)
Violet (early 20s)
Robert L. May (early 20s)

INTRO MUSIC

<u>Scene 1</u>

SANTA

991, 992, 93, 94, 95, 96, 97, 98, 99...
That's it.

MRS CLAUS

What's it, dear

SANTA

Mrs. Claus, we have reached a momentous moment in world history.

MRS. CLAUS

Oh, you've decided to stop bellowing ho, ho, ho at 3am?
That is momentous.
I've got to finish mending your hat. I don't understand how...

SANTA

Forget the hat.
Mrs. Claus, just a moment ago, the earth reached a population of 7 billion souls.

MRS. SANTA

Oh dear. How many of them are children?

SANTA

Over half I suppose.
I'll have to check the list.

MRS. CLAUS

The list? The list is the size of Rhode Island.

The Eight Plays of Christmas

Santa, how much longer can you keep this up?
Those poor little elves are exhausted, and don't get me started on the reindeer.
I just don't know…

SANTA

My dear Mrs. Claus.
You know as well I do, as long as children believe, there will always be a Santa Claus.

MRS. CLAUS

Well, it is just unfair.
Back in the 4th century AD when that Bishop Nicholas of Smyrna started this whole thing, I bet he didn't have such a workload.
How many people were there back then?

SANTA

In 400AD, about 200 million.

MRS CLAUS

Ahha!

Santa

But Nicholas of Smyrna had many duties and responsibilities as the Bishop of a newly founded Church. And he had only one helper, who at times could be most disagreeable.

MUSIC SEGUE

Scene 2

NICHOLAS

Thaddeus! Thaddeus!

THADDEUS

(off mike) What? Whadda ya want?

NICHOLAS

I need you in here.

THADDEUS

(talking and walking to mike)
Either I can get these purses done or I can chat with you.
What's it gonna be?

NICHOLAS

The purses. yes. My friend Ttitus has four daughters.
How many gold pieces did you put in each purse?

THADDEUS

Twenty. 20 for the tall daughter, 20 for the short daughter, 20 for the stout daughter and 20 for the daughter who sounds like a scalded cat when she talks.
Eighty gold pieces out of your own personal funds… and for what?

NICHOLAS

Dowries. Titus has known difficult times.
His older daughters are all of marrying age.
Without dowries, they will never find suitable mate

THADDEUS.

Hurray for Titus.
He rids himself of four daughters and you're out 80 pieces of gold.

NICHOLAS

My bounty is plenty.

The Eight Plays of Christmas

And at this time of year, I find joy in giving.

THADDEUS

"Joy in giving." You're the softest touch in Smyrna.
The whole town knows it.

NICHOLAS

It makes me happy, Thaddeus.
Oh, the bags of treats for Titus's younger children.
Are they prepared as well?

THADDEUS

(laughing throughout his lines)
Are they prepared?
Oh my, are they prepared.

NICHOLAS

What are you going on about?

THADDEUS

Your bishopness, you're going to love this.
You told the kitchen staff you would give them each a small measure of grain for their personal use for every bag of sweets they wrapped, right?

NICHOLAS

Bags of dates and nuts, yes.
So, did they do it?

THADDEUS

Did they do it?
I just finished counting how many bags of treats they did do.

NICHOLAS

How many?

THADDEUS

355! You do not have a measure of grain left in your bin.
And there's not a date or nut left in Smyrna.
What are you going to do with 355 bags of treats?

NICHOLAS

Hmm. 355 bags, 355.

THADDEUS

Why are you pacing around the room?
Titus only has five little tots.
You're stuck with 350 bags.

NICHOLAS

Thaddeus! Put all the treats in that large canvas sack we keep by the fireplace.
Have my carriage brought to the front of the rectory.

THADDEUS

What are you gonna do?

NICHOLAS

After we deliver the purses and treats to Titus, we are going to visit the homes of the poorest children in Smyrna.
We are going to place a bag of treats by each door.
They'll never know who brought them.

THADDEUS

Are you kidding?
They'll all know it's you.
Who else would do it?
And then they'll expect it next year, and the next, and the…

NICHOLAS

And we'll do it, at this time, every year.
If ever I am to have any legacy at all, I want it to be the spirit of giving…
and making children happy, all children.

THADDEUS

Legacy. What legacy?
I'm sure everyone will praise you, call you Saint Nicholas or whatever.

THADDEUS (CONT'D)

But believe me, after you're gone, the people will forget. They always do.

MUSIC: DECK THE HALLS

Scene 3

SANTA

(singing) "Fa, la, la la, la, la la, la la.
Tis, the season to be jolly.
Fa la la…

MRS. CLAUS

Santa…Santa…

SANTA

Oh, yes Mrs. Claus.

MRS. CLAUS

You do 16th century Welsh carols really well my dear.
But I kind of like the more recent songs…
songs that actually honor you.

SANTA

Actually, the spirit of Saint Nicholas journeyed through many other worthy souls before I came into being.

MRS. CLAUS

There weren't so many.
Let's see...The Saxons had King Frost, and the Vikings had Odin.
German children would wait for a visit from ChristKienlein And in France there was Pere Noel.

SANTA

English children honored Father Christmas.

MRS. SANTA

And the Dutch Settlers who first settled in New Amsterdam in the 17th century Brought Sinter Klass to America.
Now there was a jolly old soul.
He could really down a pint, I mean he…

SANTA

Yes, dear. But the spirit of Christmas almost disappeared altogether in the 17th Century.

MRS. CLAUS

Oh, you mean the Puritans.

SANTA

Can you believe 1n 1647 the Puritans forced Parliament to abolish the celebration of Christmas and Easter, in England and the Colonies.

MUSIC: GOD REST YE MERRY GENTLEMEN: KOTO KEYS – 10 SECONDS

<u>Scene 4</u>

JOHN WINTHROP

Sir! Sir! Will you please attend to me, sir?

THADDEUS

You talking to me?

JOHN WINTHROP

You are the only person standing there.

THADDEUS

Then you're talking to me.
Whadda ya want?

JOHN WINTHROP

I have been told your Bishop is away and that I must talk to the Deacon of this church.

THADDEUS

That's me, Thaddeus.
I come from a long line of deacons.
We go way back. You lookin' to marry off your daughter.
You can't do better than St. Sebastian's.
Finest church in Boston.

JOHN WINTHROP

I do not recognize saints, sir.
I am John Winthrop, Puritan Governor of Massachusets Bay Company. And I have a proclamation I want read by your Bishop at services and posted for all your parishioners to see.

THADDEUS

They can see it, but most won't be able to read it. What's it say?

JOHN WINTHROP

This proclamation is to take effect immediately in every one of the British colonies in North America.

"Forasmuch as the feast of the nativity of Christ, Easter, and other festivals, commonly called holy-days, have been heretofore superstitiously used and observed; be it ordained, that said feasts, and all other festivals, commonly called holy-days, be no longer observed as festivals. There is no day commanded in scripture to be kept holy under the gospel but the Lord's day, which is the Christian Sabbath. Festival days, vulgarly called *Holy-days*, having no warrant in the word of God, are not to be continued."

THADDEUS

That's it?

JOHN WINTHROP

I think the proclamation is perfectly clear.

THADDEUS

No celebration of Christmas.

JOHN WINTHROP

Correct.

THADDEUS

No Christmas Eve cheer? No wassail?

JOHN WINTHROP

Decidedly not.

THADDEUS
And no presents for the little ones on Christmas morning?

JOHN WINTHROP
It is totally unwarranted.

THADDEUS
Governor…Good luck with that.

MUSIC: DECK THE HALLS

<u>Scene 5</u>

MRS CLAUS
I know the spirit of Christmas suffered for a while, but by the beginning of the 19th century, you appeared my dear.

SANTA
Well, I certainly didn't look like I do now.

MRS. CLAUS
Yes, you were a bit undernourished.

SANTA
I just wasn't fleshed out yet, but that writer Washington Irving and his patron John Pintard let the people know I was around.

MUSIC:

<u>Scene 6</u>

LOUISE
Mother, father, do I have to go to bed just yet?

ELIZABETH PINTARD
Louise, all through dinner, you have bombarded Mr. Irving with your questions.

WASHINGTON IRVING
She is delightful. I have never had such a charming and knowledgeable inquisitor.

JOHN PINTARD
She has read and re-read your book since it first came out last year.

LOUISE
It's so funny. And your Christmas stories are my favorite.

ELIZABETH
And it is now Chistmas Eve.
Off to bed with you.

LOUISE (moving off mike)
Good night mother, good night father, Good night Mr. Irving.

WASHINGTON IRVING
Mrs. Pintard, It is such an enjoyable honor to spend Christmas eve in your home.
Thank you for inviting me to supper.

ELIZABETH
It is our pleasure, Mr. Irving.
And it is my honor to meet the man responsible for bringing so much joy to this season.

IRVING
Your husband John deserves most of the credit.

He was the one who encouraged me to write
Knickerbocker's History of New York and then pay
to have it published.

JOHN PINTARD

And worth every dollar.
I just wish you had used your own name.
Then Washington Irving, instead of your nom de
plume, Dietrich Knickerbocker, would be renowned
for immortalizing our daughter's most beloved spirit
of Christmas.

IRVING

Spirit of Christmas? Now who would that be?

ELIZABETH

You know very well who we mean.
When I was a little girl we all revered Saint Nicholas
as this saintly figure who watched over little children
and brought them treats at Christmastime.
But he was distant, ethereal.
Where did this Santa Claus of yours come from?

IRVING

Actually, right here in New York, from the original
Dutch settlers.
Their name for Saint Nicholas was Sinter Klass.
I just Americanized it. And when I thought about
him, this image came to mind of a jolly, rotund Dutch
burgher with a clay pipe.

JOHN

…whose horse and wagon can fly to rooftops so that
he can come down chimneys to bring gifts and fill
children's stockings, hanging at the fireplace.

ELIZABETH
Mr. Irving, please tell me we will read more of this jolly man and his sack of treats for all good children.

JOHN
Actually my dear. Mr. Irving did not just come by this evening to enjoy your excellently prepared Christmas eve supper.

The 1809 publishing of *Knickerbocker's History of New York* was so popular, we have decided to republish it.

But the 1810 edition will include a new Diedrich Nickerbocker poem featuring your favorite character.

ELIZABETH
Oh. Do you have it with you? Will you read it, please?

IRVING
I do have it with me, but I do not feel my voice would do it justice.

It should be read by a woman, as if reading to her child.

Mrs. Pintard, would you do me the honor?

ELIZABETH
It would be my pleasure, Mr. Irving.

MUSIC: "AWAY IN A MANGER" UNDERSCORES ENTIRE POEM

ELIZABETH
"Oh good holy man! whom we Santa Claus name,
The Nursery forever your praise shall proclaim:
The day of your joyful revisit returns,
When each little bosom with gratitude burns,

The Eight Plays of Christmas

For the gifts which at night you so kindly impart
To the girls of your love, and the boys of your heart.
Oh! come with your panniers and pockets well stow'd,
Our stockings shall help you to lighten your load,
As close to the fireside gaily they swing,
While delighted we dream of the presents you bring.
Oh! bring the bright Orange so juicy and sweet,
Bring almonds and raisins to heighten the treat;
Rich waffles and dough-nuts must not be forgot,
Nor Crullers and Oley-Cooks fresh from the pot.
But of all these fine presents your Saintship can find,
Oh! leave not the famous big Cookies behind.
Or if in your hurry one thing you mislay,
Let that be the Rod—and oh! keep it away.
Then holy St. Nicholas! all the year,
Our books we will love and our parents revere,
From naughty behavior we'll always refrain,
In hopes that you'll come and reward us again."

MUSIC: AWAY IN A MANGER CONTINUES INTO SCENE 6

<u>Scene 7</u>

MRS. CLAUS

Oh, what a lovely thought.

SANTA

It is a beautiful poem.

MRS. CLAUS

I am referring to Santa's wagon drawn by just one horse, Instead of that herd of reindeer the elves and I have to tend to.

SANTA

My dear, Washington Irving's vision of me became so popular and widespread during the early 19th century, he was bound to inspire other writers.
That is how I became who I am today.

MRS. CLAUS

Well that college professor Clement Clarke Moore became a little too inspired when he decided to turn your wagon into a sleigh and had eight flying reindeer pulling it. He even named them.

SANTA

My dear, *Twas the Night Before Christmas* is a classic, an utter classic.

MRS. CLAUS

I know dear, but does it always have to sound like it was written in 1823.

SANTA

What do you mean?

MRS. CLAUS

Well, the elves and I have come up with a rendition that we feel is more in keeping with modern times.

SANTA

You haven't changed the poem have you?

MRS. CLAUS

No dear, we have just added a bit of a beat to it.

The Eight Plays of Christmas

MUSIC: *TWAS THE NIGHT BEFORE CHRISTMAS*, ADAPTED AND RECORDED BY BRYANT ODEN.

"Twas the night before Christmas, when all through the house
Not a creature was stirring, not even a mouse.
The stockings were hung by the chimney with care,
In hopes that St Nicholas soon would be there.
The children were nestled all snug in their beds,
While visions of sugar-plums danced in their heads.
And mamma in her 'kerchief, and I in my cap,
Had just settled our brains for a long winter's nap.
When out on the lawn there arose such a clatter,
I sprang from the bed to see what was the matter.
Away to the window I flew like a flash,
Tore open the shutters and threw up the sash.
The moon on the breast of the new-fallen snow
Gave the lustre of mid-day to objects below.
When, what to my wondering eyes should appear,
But a miniature sleigh, and eight tinny reindeer.
With a little old driver, so lively and quick,
I knew in a moment it must be St Nick.
More rapid than eagles his coursers they came,
And he whistled, and shouted, and called them by name!
"Now Dasher! now, Dancer! now, Prancer and Vixen!
On, Comet! On, Cupid! on, on Donner and Blitzen!
To the top of the porch! to the top of the wall!
Now dash away! Dash away! Dash away all!"
As dry leaves that before the wild hurricane fly,
When they meet with an obstacle, mount to the sky.
So up to the house-top the coursers they flew,
With the sleigh full of Toys, and St Nicholas too.
And then, in a twinkling, I heard on the roof
The prancing and pawing of each little hoof.
As I drew in my head, and was turning around,

Down the chimney St Nicholas came with a bound.
He was dressed all in fur, from his head to his foot,
And his clothes were all tarnished with ashes and soot.
A bundle of Toys he had flung on his back,
And he looked like a peddler, just opening his pack.
His eyes-how they twinkled! his dimples how merry!
His cheeks were like roses, his nose like a cherry!
His droll little mouth was drawn up like a bow,
And the beard of his chin was as white as the snow.
The stump of a pipe he held tight in his teeth,
And the smoke it encircled his head like a wreath.
He had a broad face and a little round belly,
That shook when he laughed, like a bowlful of jelly!
He was chubby and plump, a right jolly old elf,
And I laughed when I saw him, in spite of myself!
A wink of his eye and a twist of his head,
Soon gave me to know I had nothing to dread.
He spoke not a word, but went straight to his work,
And filled all the stockings, then turned with a jerk.
And laying his finger aside of his nose,
And giving a nod, up the chimney he rose!
He sprang to his sleigh, to his team gave a whistle,
And away they all flew like the down of a thistle.
But I heard him exclaim, 'ere he drove out of sight,
"Happy Christmas to all, and to all a good-night!"

SANTA

Well, that is the fastest version I've ever heard.

MRS. CLAUS

We are living in swifter times, Santa, all 7 billion of us.

SANTA

It makes me appreciate the attention to Christmas that was given as America was growing.

The Eight Plays of Christmas

And I must credit that amazing artist Thomas Nast who finally created the lasting image of me in his illustrations for Harper's Magazine during the 1860s.

MRS. CLAUS

But did he have to add such details as Santa's workshop being at the North Pole and Santa's list of the good and bad children, which as I've told you is…

SANTA

…as big as Rhode Island. I know.

MRS. CLAUS

Well, his illustrations were inspirational.
It was one of Nast's images of you that young Virginia O'Hanlon had on her wall when she wrote her letter to the New York Sun in 1897. And it was reporter Francis P Church's editorial reply on September 21, 1897 that carried your presence into the 20th century.

MUSIC: SILENT NIGHT/HAVE YOURSELF A MERRY LITTLE CHRISTMAS

<u>Scene 8</u>

VIRGINIA

Dear Editor, I am 8 years old. Some of my little friends say there is no Santa Claus. Papa says, "If you see it in The Sun, it's so." Please tell me the truth, is there a Santa Claus? - Virginia O'Hanlon.

CHURCH

Virginia, your little friends are wrong. They have been affected by the skepticism of a skeptical age. They do not believe except [what] they see. They think that nothing can be which is not comprehensible by their little minds. All minds, Virginia, whether they be men's or children's, are little. In this great universe of ours, man is a mere insect, an ant, in his intellect as compared with the boundless world about him, as measured by the intelligence capable of grasping the whole of truth and knowledge.

Yes, Virginia, there is a Santa Claus. He exists as certainly as love and generosity and devotion exist, and you know that they abound and give to your life its highest beauty and joy. Alas! how dreary would be the world if there were no

Santa Claus! It would be as dreary as if there were no Virginias. There would be no childlike faith then, no poetry, no romance to make tolerable this existence. We should have no enjoyment, except in sense and sight. The external light with which childhood fills the world would be extinguished.

Not believe in Santa Claus! You might as well not believe in fairies. You might get your papa to hire men to watch in all the chimneys on Christmas eve to catch Santa Claus, but even if you did not see Santa Claus coming down, what would that prove? Nobody sees Santa Claus, but that is no sign that there is no Santa Claus. The most real things in the world are those that neither children nor men can see. Did you ever see fairies dancing on the lawn? Of course not, but that's no proof that they are not there. Nobody can conceive or imagine all the wonders there are unseen and unseeable in the world.

The Eight Plays of Christmas

You may tear apart the baby's rattle and see what makes the noise inside, but there is a veil covering the unseen world which not the strongest man, nor even the united strength of all the strongest men that ever lived could tear apart. Only faith, fancy, poetry, love, romance, can push aside that curtain and view and picture the supernal beauty and glory beyond. Is it all real? Ah, Virginia, in all this world there is nothing else [more] real and abiding.

No Santa Claus! Thank God! he lives and lives forever. A thousand years from now, Virginia, nay 10 times 10,000 years from now, he will continue to make glad the heart of childhood. Your humble servant, Francis P. Church.

MUSIC: HAVE YOURSELF A MERRY LITTLE CHRISTMAS –

<u>Scene 9</u>

SANTA

The 20th century was so difficult. I am so glad we are beyond it. The industrialization…the wars…the unrelenting grasping for wealth. Truth and goodness seemed to disappear. Life became one big advertising campaign.

MRS CLAUS

I like the holiday ads, the funny jingles. You are certainly prominent.

SANTA

Prominent? They turned me into a huckster.

MRS. CLAUS

Well, I didn't mind the Coca Cola illustrations of you created by that lovely artist, Haddon Sundblom in 1931. He made you life-sized. Before that, you were about the size of one of your elves. He turned you into the fine, robust figure you are today.

SANTA

True. But you weren't happy at all with the holiday ad campaign the Montgomery Ward Company put out in 1939.

MRS. CLAUS

Of course, I wasn't happy. It was hard enough dealing with eight self-centered reindeer. Then that wet-behind-his-ears ad writer Robert L. May had to create a ninth.

MUSIC: SILVER BELLS

<u>Scene 10</u>

VIOLET

Robert…Robert…where are you going?

ROBERT

I'm done. The Montgomery Ward campaign is ready to go.
I'm headed for Pete's Tavern. All the copywriters are meeting there. Get your coat. Let's go.

VIOLET

I can't go anywhere. And neither can you.
We're not finished yet.

ROBERT

I am. The ad copy has been written, edited and approved. The art's been O.K'd.
It's all being shipped to the printer in the morning. The only thing we're waiting on is the coloring book that Montgomery Ward selects every year to give away at the stores. And that is not our department.

VIOLET

It is now. The store has decided that purchasing coloring books is too expensive. They want to create their own

ROBERT

And have it ready to ship to the printer by tomorrow? Who's the poor soul idiot that's gonna write it?

VIOLET

You.

ROBERT

What? No!

VIOLET

And I'm the poor soul idiot who has to illustrate it. So if you want us both to keep our jobs in these Depression times, we better get to work.

ROBERT

Oh boy! All right, you have to do the illustrations, so what are you good at drawing?

VIOLET

Robert, I am a great illustrator. I can draw anything. Although, I have had a lot of practice lately doing reindeer, lots of reindeer.

ROBERT

Fine. The lead character is going to be one of Santa's reindeer.

VIOLET

Which one?

ROBERT

Let's be creative. We'll invent a new one.
It's name should start with an "R" to go along with reindeer. How about Rollo the Reindeer?

VIOLET

I don't think so. How about Reginald?

ROBERT

Too hoity toity. Maybe Rudolph?

VIOLET

Actually, I have an uncle named Rudolph. What a boozer.
When he gets drunk, his nose turns so bright red, I swear he could find his way out of a darkened room.

ROBERT

Hilarious! Get serious. We have to find a plot for this…
Whoa…whoa…whoa…"nose so bright."…

VIOLET

What's wrong?

ROBERT

Violet, get out your sketch pad.
We've got our coloring book.

SONG RECORDING: "Rudolph The Red-Nosed Reindeer"

Scene 11

SANTA

Rudolph has become so popular over the years: a book, a hit song, TV, movies

MRS. CLAUS

My dear, he's become a superstar.

THADDEUS

And don't he know it. He thinks he's king of the stable. O.k. folks, we ready to go here? Everything is on the sleigh and the reindeer are pointed due south.

SANTA

Thaddeus, you've been part of this from the very beginning.

THADDEUS

Yeah, well without me around, they'd turn Christmas into an App. Let's get this show on the road.

SANTA

Well dear. I'm off. I will return by dawn.

MRS. CLAUS

And as always, I will make my toddy, play my favorite music and wait for your return.

SANTA

(moving off mike) Merry Christmas to all…Ho, Ho, Ho.

The End

KEEPING CHRISTMAS WELL

(THE MAKING OF A CHRISTMAS CAROL)

Written By Julio Martinez

Narrator (any age)
Mr. Warren/Scrooge (mid 50s)
Mrs. Roylance/Maid (mid 30s)
Young Charles Dickens/Lad (12 years old)
Washington Irving/Bob Cratchit (mid 30s)
Charles Dickens (early 30s)
Mrs. Catherine Dickens (early 30s)
Prince Albert/Fred (mid 20s)
Queen Victoria/Fred's wife (Mid 20s)
Mrs. Fanny Kemble (early 30s)

Scene 1

NARRATOR
On 20 February 1824, John Dickens, a competent London clerk possessing very little competency with his finances, is confined to Marshalsea Prison, pursuant to the Insolvent Debtor's Act of 1813, due to arrears in the amount of 40 pounds and 10 shillings owed to a baker, Mr. James Kerr. This is certainly bad news for his wife Elizabeth and the three younger of his eight children who are forced to join him at

Marshalsea. But none suffers as much consternation as 12-year-old Charles Dickens, a scholarly lad who is pursuing his studies, while being boarded at the home of an elderly family friend, Mrs. Roylance, in Camden Town.

THE SOUND OF SEVERE POUNDING ON A DOOR

MR. WARREN

Master Charles Dickens, I know you are in there. Attend me at once.

MRS. ROYLANCE

I am sure the lad is still sleeping, sir. He studies late into the night.

CONTINUING TO POUND ON DOOR.

MR. WARREN

Studies! Bah! Humbug! Master Charles Dickens, open this door.

SOUND OF DOOR OPENING

YOUNG DICKENS

Sir?

MR. WARREN

Am I in the presence of Charles Dickens, son of John Dickens, currently residing in Marshalsea Prison, due to unresolved financial arrears?

YOUNG DICKENS

Yes, sir.

MR. WARREN

Correct! Young man, you are to gather your belongings and come with me. You are changing your place of residence.

YOUNG DICKENS

But sir, I reside with Mrs. Roylance until I complete my studies.

MR. WARREN

Studies! Humbug and more humbug.
From this moment, you are gainfully employed at Warren's Blacking Warehouse, where you will earn six shillings a week, which I consider an extravagance, since you possess no employable skills, which I promise you, will be rectified.

YOUNG DICKENS

But I….

MRS. ROYLANCE

Master Charles, your mother has no choice but to contract you out to Mr. Warren to help alleviate your family's dire situation.

MR. WARREN

And I have taken valuable time from my workday to fetch you. Now, snap to it.

YOUNG DICKENS

Excuse me, sir. It will take me a moment to gather my books.

MRS. ROYLANCE

Oh Charles, I am sorry. Your mother has given me instructions to sell your books. The funds are needed to help sustain your brothers and sisters. Mr. Warren has arranged for a bookseller to come around this very day.

YOUNG DICKENS
Please, not my books…..

MRS. ROYLANCE
Mr. Warren, let the lad at least keep one.

MR. WARREN
Bah! So be it. I've always been a soft touch for the ladies. It has been the ruin of me. Take a book and be done with it.

YOUNG DICKENS
I guess I'll bring this one: *Bracebridge Hall*. It is by Mr. Washington Irving from America. I haven't had a chance yet to read it.

MR. WARREN
Hmph! I promise you master Dickens, after you have suffered a day of honest labor at my establishment, you won't have the strength to read.

Scene 2

NARRATOR
Mr. Warren is good to his word. Young Charles Dickens toils through 10-hour workdays with only Sunday serving as a reprieve. For his earned six shillings, the lad relentlessly pastes labels on pots of boot blacking. The strenuous and often punishing working conditions he suffers makes a lasting impression on young Dickens.

What Mr. Warren does not predict is the voracious need of his young employee to devour any reading material that comes his way no matter how exhausted he is from his labours.

The novel by Washington Irving is his constant companion.

After a year of servitude, young Dickens is allowed to leave the employ of Mr. Warren.

MRS ROYLANCE
(SINGING) "The holly and the ivy,
When they are full grown,
Of all trees that in the wood,
The holly bears the crown;
O, the rising of the sun,
And the running of the deer
The playing of the merry organ,
Sweet singing in the choir…"

YOUNG DICKENS
Mrs. Roylance.

MRS ROYLANCE
(STARTLED) Oh, my gracious.

YOUNG DICKENS
It is Charles Dickens.

MRS ROYLANCE
Master Charles. What a pleasure.
Let me put my laundry down and have a look at you.
How long has it been?

The Eight Plays of Christmas

YOUNG DICKENS

A year, mam. My father has been released from Marshalsea and is now gainfully employed.
I have been allowed to return to school.
I am to attend Willington House Academy in North London.

MRS ROYLANCE

All the better for you, master Charles.
A lad with your mind should not be confined to a workhouse.
I prayed every day that you were at least safe.

YOUNG DICKENS

Mrs Roylance, what I witnessed and experienced there will haunt me the rest of my life.
That is why I am here, to thank you…for this.

MRS ROYLANCE

A book?

YOUNG DICKENS

Yes! *Bracebridge Hall* was my salvation.
You intervened on my behalf so I could keep it.
The author, Mr Irving, has quite an imagination.
He is an American, but writes so beautifully of English life and about joyous Christmastime at a country manor house.
I have never known Christmas to be anything but a reminder of how difficult life can be.

MRS ROYLANCE

Oh master Charles. You never lived in the countryside as I did when a young girl. My father worked in the grainery of a large manor. The work was hard. But on

Christmas Eve, the squire – oh what I fat jolly man he was – would gather all his workers around him and shout, 'No more work today, lads.
It's Christmas. It's Christmas.' What comical figures the squire and his wife were during the dancing; and what joy he gave to everyone in his employ.
There was feasting and games and presents for all the children.
I wish you lived in happier times.
Master Charles Dickens, I wish you all the success and the happiness you deserve.

Scene 3

NARRATOR

Through the ensuing two decades, Charles Dickens acquires more than success; he is esteemed as the most accomplished literary figure of his time, publishing such treasured works as *Oliver Twist*, *Nicholas Nickleby*, *Pickwick Papers* and *The Old Curiosity Shop*, all before the age of 30. As for happiness, he finds it in the personage of Catherine Thomson Hogarth, whom he marries on 2 April 1836; and who eventually bears him ten children.
Also finding happiness in marriage is England's sovereign, youthful Queen Victoria, who weds 20-year-old Prince Albert of Saxony on 10 February 1840.
But by December, Victoria's prince is not so delighted to be living in the dour environment of the royal palace.

PRINCE ALBERT

Dies ist nicht, wie man Weihnachten feiern.
Dies ist nicht, wie man Weihnachten feiern.
Dies ist nicht,

The Eight Plays of Christmas

QUEEN VICTORIA

In English, my husband, please. In English, my dear.

ALBERT

My wife...my Queen.
Why are there no plans to celebrate the day of our savior's birth?

VICTORIA

We do. The royal family always sets an example by going to church on Christmas day.

PRINCE

Church is not celebration. It is duty.
Where are the decorations, the music, the feasting, the joy?

VICTORIA

Oh! Is that necessary?

PRINCE

It is in my home. Is this not my home?

VICTORIA

This is your home, forever, my husband.
I am your queen; but you are master in this house.

PRINCE

Gut!

MUSIC: HAIL BRITANNIA

NARRATOR

It isn't long before all of London society becomes witness to Prince Albert's influence on palace life and on the city as well. Meanwhile, in 1842, Charles and Catherine Dickens make their first visit to America; and during a one-month stay in New York, are hosted by the literary hero of Dickens' youth, Mr. Washington Irving.

DICKENS
My dear, I can truthfully say that I did not retire two nights out of seven without taking Washington Irving under my arm upstairs to bed with me.

CATHERINE
I should be jealous but I am not.
I applaud my husband's taste in all matters.

IRVING
I also applaud your husband, madame.
It is a great honor for me to have inspired Charles Dickens in any way. I have read all your works sir. And since you have barely reached your 30th year, I look forward to many more works to come.

DICKENS
And if there are any characters from my works you wish to amplify with your genius, you have my hearty approval.
After all, without Washington Irving's *Bracebridge Hall*, there would have been no Charles Dickens' *Pickwick Papers*.

CATHERINE
Is this true? You mean all those lovely recreations of country manor Christmas celebrations in *Pickwick Papers* did not come purely out of your own imagination, my dear?

DICKENS

My dear, you must read *Bracebridge Hall.*
You will see that the merry Olde England Christmas celebrations that *Pickwick Papers* so inadequately chronicled in 1837, were more joyously created by our American friend, Mr. Irving in 1822.

IRVING

I was fortunate enough to travel through all of Europe during that time; but I was privileged to spend many months in your English countryside, taking notes on your ancient traditions, rituals and customs.
And at no time were they celebrated with greater aplomb than at Christmas.

CATHERINE

Charles, why not leave the English countryside to Mr. Irving.
My dear, no one knows London town better than you. Why don't you write about London and its Christmas traditions.

DICKENS

Traditions? Catherine, Mr. Irving, when I was 20, I became a journalist with the London Morning Chronicle.
I observed first hand the lives of men, women, and children in the most impoverished areas of London and have borne witness to the social injustices they have suffered.
I trust my novels have been entertaining; but they have also been indictments of the inhuman industrialization of city life that renders Christmas just another 24 hours of tedious survival for much of the population.

CATHERINE

But Charles, I have noticed a change in attitudes about Christmas in London ever since our Queen Victoria married the Saxon Prince Albert.

I am told he is introducing the German tradition of decorating a tree, inside Windsor Palace.

All of London is abuzz about it, Charles.

IRVING

It is a charming German tradition turning a simple evergreen into a glorious representation of Christmas. In the German Village of Ulm, I witnessed the whole community decorating a massive fir tree, festooning it with candles, ribbons, fruits, nuts and at the top there was placed a carving of the star that guided the wise men.

CATHERINE

Charles, if you put your mind and talent to it, I believe you could combine your desire to right the wrongs in our society while also displaying the true spirit of Christmas and the joy it can bring to peoples' lives, especially the less fortunate among us.

I know London society is going through great changes in this modern age, but I believe it also yearns for the times of old when life was simpler and Christmas was the most glorious day of the year.

IRVING

Well, Mr Charles Dickens, the gauntlet has been thrown by the most important member of your household.

Are you up to it?

Scene 4

NARRATOR

Upon his return to England at the beginning of 1843, Charles Dickens does not take up the challenge put forward by his wife. Instead, he heeds a request by the 84-member Children's Employment Commission to personally investigate reports of slave-like conditions in the tin mines at Cornwall, particularly for children.

DICKENS

Catherine, what I saw has strengthened my resolve even further to devote the rest of the year to writing and promoting a pamphlet titled, 'An appeal to the people of England, on behalf of the poor man's child.'

CATHERINE

Husband, I do believe this pamphlet you plan to spend so much of your time writing and promoting is a noble effort and very important to society, but...

DICKENS

But what, my dear?

CATHERINE

Will it earn you any money

DICKENS

Very little, actually. But I will still be able to provide for my family.

CATHERINE

That is my point, Charles.
Your family will soon be getting a wee bit larger.

DICKENS

Another one?

CATHERINE

Yes dear.

DICKENS

I see. Yes, I do see. Yes, indeed.

CATHERINE

My dear, why are you pacing?

DICKENS

(TO HIMSELF) Humbug, bah humbug indeed. This can work, yes I think…

CATHERINE

Charles! What are you mumbling about?

DICKENS

Catherine, in the morning will you please lay out my striped trousers, maroon waistcoat, black frocked coat and my high hat?

CATHERINE

That can only mean you are going to pay a visit to your publishers, Chapman and Hall.

DICKENS

Very astute my dear. The pamphlet will have to wait. I have been thinking about this for awhile.
I am going to petition my publishers to give me a percentage of profits from my next book rather than the lump sum paid to me in the past.
As my family grows, so must my income.

CATHERINE

So you know what your next book will be?

DICKENS

Yes, my dear. Not so long ago I was petitioned by a very persuasive individual to write a book about Christmas that was reflective of life in London.

CATHERINE

Oh Charles, I am so happy.
Do you know what the plot will be?

DICKENS

Observing the wretched conditions of the poor children working in the mines at Cornwall brought back the ghost of my Christmas past when, for a time, I was forced to suffer their plight.
I began to ponder how I could invent a character who embodied both the misery of life's often cruel realities and the joy of Christmas's glorious promise.

CATHERINE

My goodness, husband. That would be quite a feat.
Have you come up with an answer to your pondering?

DICKENS

Yes, my dear. I do believe I have

Scene 5

NARRATOR

Charles Dickens begins to put pen to paper in September 1843.
Writing in a fury of inspiration and financial necessity, he completes the final pages in early December.
A Christmas Carol is published on 19 December.

The novella achieves immediate success far beyond its author's expectations. The acclaimed writer William Makepeace Thackery declares the book, 'a national benefit and to every man or woman who reads it, a personal kindness.'

The novella is immediately adapted for the stage by noted actor and theatre manager, Edward Stirling, whose annual productions are sanctioned by Dickens. At a dinner party, celebrating the 10th anniversary of the publication of *A Christmas Carol*, hosted by Charles and Catherine, Stirling and members of his company are moved to offer the final scene in the salvation and re-birth of Ebenezer Scrooge.

STIRLING
With your permission, sir.

DICKENS
You most wholeheartedly have it, Mr. Stirling.

STIRLING
Mistress Fanny Kemble, are the players at the ready?

FANNY KEMBLE
They are indeed, sir. Places everyone.

MUSIC

STIRLING/SCROOGE
"Am I that man who lay upon the bed? No, Spirit! O no, no! Spirit! hear me! I am not the man I was. I will not be the man I must have been but for this intercourse. Why show me this, if I am past all hope? Assure me that I yet

STIRLING/SCROOGE (CONT'D)

may change these shadows you have shown me by an altered life."

FANNY

For the first time the phantom's hand faltered.

STIRLING/SCROOGE

"I will honor Christmas in my heart, and try to keep it all the year. I will live in the Past, the Present, and the Future. The Spirits of all three shall strive within me. I will not shut out the lessons that they teach. O, tell me I may sponge away the writing on this stone!"

FANNY

Holding up his hands in one last prayer to have his fate reversed, he saw an alteration in the Phantom's hood and dress. It shrunk, collapsed, and dwindled down into a bedpost.

STIRLING/SCROOGE

Yes, the bedpost is my own. The bed is my own, the room is my own. Best and happiest of all, the Time before me is my own, to make amends in!

THE SOUND OF BELLS PEALING

The bells. I must look out the window. No fog, no mist, no night; a clear, bright, stirring, golden day. There's a lad. Boy! Oh, boy!

LAD

Eh?

STIRLING/SCROOGE

What's to-day, my fine fellow?

LAD

To-day! Why, Christmas Day.

STIRLING/SCROOGE

It's Christmas day! I haven't missed it. Hallo, my fine fellow!"

LAD

Hallo!

STIRLING/SCROOGE

Do you know the poulterer in the next street, at the corner?

LAD

I should hope I did.

STIRLING/SCROOGE

An intelligent boy! A remarkable boy! Do you know whether they've sold the prize Turkey that was hanging up there? Not the little prize Turkey, -- the big one?

LAD

What, the one as big as me?

STIRLING/SCROOGE

What a delightful boy! It's a pleasure to talk to him. Yes, my buck!"

LAD

It's hanging there now.

STIRLING/SCROOGE

Is it? Go and buy it.

LAD
Walk-er!

STIRLING/SCROOGE
No, no, I am in earnest. Go and buy it, and tell 'em to bring it here, that I may give them the direction where to take it. Come back with the man, and I'll give you a shilling. Come back with him in less than five minutes, and I'll give you half a crown!"

LAD
Right, yes sir!

STIRLING/SCROOGE
I'll send it to Bob Cratchit's! He sha'n't know who sends it. It's twice the size of Tiny Tim. Joe Miller never made such a joke as sending it to Bob's will be!"

FANNY
Scrooge dressed himself "all in his best," and at last got out into the streets. The people were by this time pouring forth through the streets.

AN AURAL COLLAGE OF SCROOGE AND PASSERSBY AS HE MAKE HIS WAY THROUGH THE STREETS OF LONDON ON HIS WAY TO HIS NEPHEW'S HOUSE

STIRLING/SCROOGE
Merry Christmas. Good morning, Merry Christmas to you, etc., etc.

ENSEMBLE
Merry Christmas to you, sir. Good morning. Happy Christmas time to you, etc, etc

STIRLING/SCROOGE

Oh my, oh my, where am I now? It's my nephew's house. Fred! I don't know if I have the nerve. I must. I must knock.

A KNOCK ON THE DOOR

MAID

Good day, sir.

STIRLING/SCROOGE

Is your master at home, my dear?

MAID

Yes, sir.

STIRLING/SCROOGE

Where is he, my love?

MAID

He's in the dining-room, sir, with his mistress.

STIRLING/SCROOGE

He knows me. I'll go in here, my dear. (TO FRED) Fred!

FRED

Why, bless my soul! Who's that?

STIRLING/SCROOGE

It's I, Your uncle Scrooge. I have come to dinner. Will you let me in, Fred?"

FRED

Let you in? Oh Uncle, I have so hoped for this day. (TO HIS WIFE). My dear, look who is joining us for Christmas dinner.

STIRLING/SCROOGE

(TO FRED'S WIFE) My dear, can you find it in your heart to forgive this foolish old man?

FRED'S WIFE

Oh dearest Uncle. You have made Fred so happy. Please join us, today and every day.

FANNY

Ebenezer Scrooge lost himself in the wonderful dinner, wonderful party, wonderful games, wonderful happiness. But he was early at the office next morning. O, he was early there. If he could only be there first, and catch Bob Cratchit coming late! That was the thing he had set his heart upon.

STIRLING/SCROOGE

Oh, ho. It is now 18 minutes past the time, and he is just coming in. I must be stern now. (TO CRATCHIT) Hallo! What do you mean by coming here at this time of day?

CRATCHIT

I am very sorry, sir. I am behind my time.

STIRLING/SCROOGE

You are? Yes. I think you are. Step this way, if you please."

CRATCHIT

It's only once a year, sir. It shall not be repeated. I was making rather merry yesterday, sir.

STIRLING/SCROOGE

Now, I'll tell you what, my friend. I am not going to stand this sort of thing any longer. And therefore… and therefore I am about to raise your salary!"

CRATCHIT

Wha…?

STIRLING/SCROOGE.

A merry Christmas, Bob! A merrier Christmas, Bob, my good fellow, than I have given you for many a year! I'll raise your salary, and endeavor to assist your struggling family, and we will discuss your affairs this very afternoon, over a Christmas bowl of smoking bishop, Bob! Make up the fires, and buy a second coal-scuttle before you dot another "i," Bob Cratchit!

FANNY

Scrooge was better than his word. He did it all, and infinitely more; and to Tiny Tim, who did NOT die, he was a second father.

CRATCHIT

He became as good a friend, as good a master, and as good a man as the good old city knew, or any other good old city, town, or borough in the good old world.

FRED

And it was always said of him, that he knew how to keep Christmas well, if any man alive possessed the knowledge.

FRED'S WIFE

May that be truly said of us, and all of us! And so, as Tiny Tim observed....

STIRLING

Honored guests. Forgive the interruption. But I do believe there is only one person that should conclude this celebration of this immortal work. Mister Dickens, may I call upon you to utter the final words of this play.

DICKENS

It is my pleasure sir.
To all of us gathered here tonight, And to those everywhere who celebrate this day.
God Bless Us, Every One!

The End

THE CHRISTMAS EVE TRUCE

Written by Julio Martinez

Emily Hobhouse, British, mid-50s
Rosa Mayreder, Austrian, mid-50s
Bruce Bairnsfather, British, late-20s
Bill, Scottish, mid-40s
Corporal Phillip Frings, German, 20
Captain Sir Edward Hulse, British, early 30s

INTRO MUSIC – ANGELS WE HAVE HEARD ON HIGH

EMILY HOBHOUSE

To our sisters in peace, Emily Hobhouse, London. On this 1st day of December, 1914 - Peace on earth, goodwill towards men.
As a devoted member of the British Suffragettes, I offer a Christmas greeting to the Suffragette women of Germany and Austria.
The Christmas message sounds like mockery to a world at war, but those of us who wished and still wish for peace may surely offer a solemn greeting to such of you who feel as we do. Is it not our mission to preserve life?
Do not humanity and common sense alike prompt us to join hands with the women of neutral countries, and urge our rulers to stay further bloodshed?
Even through the clash of arms, we treasure our poet Shelly's vision, and already seem to hear "a hundred nations swear that there shall be pity and peace among the good and free."

By the common striving for the highest object - personal and political freedom - may Christmas hasten that day.

ROSA MAYREDER

From your sister in peace, Rosa Mayreder, Vienna.

To our English sisters, we express, in the name of many Austrian and German women, our warm and heartfelt thanks, due to your Christmas greetings, which we only heard of lately.

This message was a confirmation of what we foresaw – that women of the belligerent countries, with all faithfulness, devotion, and love to their country, can go beyond it and maintain true solidarity with the women of other belligerent nations, and that really civilized women never lose their humanity.

On December 1, my fellow Austrian sisters in peace petitioned his reverence Pope Benedict to intervene for a truce as we approach the holiest of days. On this day December 7, we are joyful that his reverence has begged the warring nations for such a truce, asking "that – at least upon the night the angel sang, Christmas Eve - the guns may fall silent."

A COLLAGE OF BOMB, ROCKET AND MACHINE GUN FIRE

BILL

(YELLING)
Are you stupid, man?
Jump in the trench before the Bosche blow your head off.

BRUCE BAIRNSFATHER

Uhhh!
Thank you. Oh my God, this hole smells like bloody hell.

BILL

Well, if you know of a better 'ole, go to it. I'm sure the Bosche will wait for you to make proper accommodations.

BRUCE

How long have you been here?

BILL

They have been shooting for three hours. I've been in this trench for three hours. Where did you come from, laddie?

BRUCE

Royal Warwickshire Regiment... We just arrived.

BILL

Just in time to spend Christmas Eve with a regiment of Huns just a hundred yards away, all primed to send us both to kingdom come. Do you come by a name?
2

BRUCE

Bruce...Bruce Bairnsfather.
You're right. Today is Christmas Eve. You're Scottish?

BILL

Did my accent give me away?
My name's Bill.
The Gordon Highlanders have been my regiment for 20 years now.

BRUCE

Oh, a career soldier. What is your rank?

BILL

I've been promoted and demoted so many times, I've lost track. When I last looked at my arm, there were sergeant stripes.

THERE IS A LULL IN THE BARRAGE.

BRUCE
Bill, the Germans have stopped shooting.

BILL
If you want them to start up again, just stick your head up out of this hole. It is getting too dark for them and for us. It'll all start up again at dawn.

BRUCE
On Christmas day.

BILL
War has no religion, laddie.

BRUCE
They're so close to us.
I can hear them talking sometimes. I'm sure they can hear us.

BILL
Well, then, let's give them something to listen to. (BELLOWING) "Silent night, holy night. All is calm All is bright Round Young virgin, mother and child. Holy infant so tender and mild. Sleep in heavenly peace, Sleep in heavenly peace."
That should settle them Bosche down for the night.

BRUCE
I'm not so sure.

GERMAN SOLDIERS SINGING FROM A DISTANCE
"Stille Nacht, heilige Nacht,

BRUCE
Bill! Listen! Listen!

GERMAN SOLDIERS CONTINUING

"Alles schläft; einsam wacht
Nur das traute hochheilige Paar.
Holder Knabe im lockigen Haar,
Schlaf in himmlischer Ruh! Schlaf in himmlischer Ruh!

INTERMITTENTLY, WHILE THE GERMANS ARE SINGING, BILL AND BRUCE TALK

BRUCE

Bill, are the Germans singing to us?

BILL

Well, they're certainly not shooting.

BRUCE

If they're singing, it means they're celebrating Christmas.

BILL

It means nothing of the kind.
I could mow down a whole platoon of Bosche
While singing 'Comin Through the Rye.'
(SHOUTING TO GERMANS) And a happy New Year to you too.

THE GERMAN SOLDIERS STOP SINGING. BRUCE STANDS UP

BRUCE

Don't stop. Keep singing.

GERMANS RESUME SINGING. BILL YANKS HIM DOWN, TALK OVER SINGING

BILL

You want to get yourself killed.
Then you'll surely know 'Silent Night.'"

BRUCE

But this has to mean something.

BILL

They're probably shellshocked and don't know any better. But we do. Keep your head down.

BRUCE

Bill, I hear someone crawling this way.

BILL

From our side of the lines,
But we take no chances. (SHOUTING) Who goes there?

CAPTAIN SIR EDWARD HULSE CRAWLS INTO THEIR TRENCH CAPTAIN HULSE
Friend. Ugh. Bairnsfather!

BRUCE

Captain Hulse.
Sir, are we moving forward?

CAPTAIN HULSE

Nobody is moving anywhere.
The Germans are from the 134th Saxon Regiment.
Our reconnaissance informs us they are digging more trenches. They are going to be here for awhile and so are we.
(TO BILL) Sergeant, where is your regiment?

BILL

I am not too sure of that, Captain.
I got pinned down by the Huns.
I think it was fate I was left behind to keep young Bruce here from getting himself killed.

BRUCE

Captain, the Germans were singing *Silent Night.* It was beautiful.

CORPORAL PHILIP FRINGS

(FROM A DSTANCE) British soldiers. British soldiers. Please do not shoot. May I talk to you., My name is Corporal Philip Frings. I am translator.
I am unarmed. Please, may we talk.

BILL

I see him. He's coming at us like he's crossin' the heather on a spring day. He's daft.

CAPTAIN HULSE CALLS OUT

CAPTAIN HULSE

Stay where you are.I am Captain Hulse.
I am coming forward with two of my men.

BILL

Now, what two men could that be?

BRUCE

I think he means us.

BILL

Oh, you're a bright laddie you are.

CAPTAIN HULSE

Let's go. And leave your weapons.

BILL

I was afraid you were going to say that, Captain. Well, if it's my time, it's my time.

Up you go, Bruce my lad.

BRUCE
Don't push.

PHILLIP FRINGS IS TALKING AS THE THREE BRITISH SOLDIERS APPROACH. HIS VOICE GETTING MORE PRESENT UNTIL ALL THE MEN ARE TOGETHER.

CORPORAL FRINGS
I repeat. I am unarmed. I am a translator who has lived in your country.

CAPTAIN HULSE
It does appear he's not carrying a weapon. (TO FRINGS) How old are you?

CORPORAL FRINGS
I am 20.

BRUCE
Oh, were you in university...

CAPTAIN HULSE
So, Corporal Frings. Can you tell me why we are all standing here in the middle of a battlefield on Christmas Eve?

CORPORAL FRINGS
Captain, Most of the men in our regiment are young, like me. Many are not yet 20 years of age. They are homesick.
They are very frightened. Christmas is a sacred time.
We desire to light candles to give us some memory of home. But we are afraid if we light the candles, you will shoot at us.

Julio Martinez

My family is from Stuttgard. My father is still there. But my mother raised me in your country, in Suffolk. My fiancé is there. She and I will be married next year after this fighting is over. She is waiting. I leave my motorcycle with her. I miss my motorcycle very much.

BRUCE

Corporal, we heard singing coming from your men.

CORPORAL FRINGS

Yes. We have a platoon of young men from Austria in our regiment. They are from Oberndorf. They sing in the church choir.
We hear someone trying to sing from your side and they want to help.

BILL

Help! I don't need any help.

CAPTAIN HULSE

Corporal, may I meet these young men from Oberndorf?

CORPORAL FRINGS

Certainly Captain.

CORPORAL FRINGS WALKS AWAY

BRUCE

Captain, what can you do?

CAPTAIN HULSE

Nothing really. I cannot go to command headquarters and request we don't shoot at the enemy.

SOUND OF MEN WALKING

CORPORAL FRINGS

Captain, these are the men I was referring to. They don't speak English.

CAPTAIN HULSE

Well, my men say they can sing. I would like to hear them.

CORPORAL FRINGS

Of course.
(TO THE CHORUS) Bitte?

GERMAN SOLDIERS BEGIN SINGING ANOTHER CHRISTMAS BALLAD. DURING THE SINGING THE FOLLOWING DIALOGUE CONTINUES.

CAPTAIN HULSE

This is magnificent

BRUCE

Captain, Bill...look.
The Germans are leaving the trenches.
They're coming this way. Some of them are holding candles.

CAPTAIN HULSE

I'm not blind, private. I see them, too.

BILL

I know I'm not blind, but I must be dreaming.
Our men have left their trenches. They're coming this way, too.

BRUCE

They're holding candles.

Julio Martinez

BILL
Captain, Bruce my lad.
It has never happened before.
It won't happen again. But we are having a Christmas Truce.

THERE IS 10 SECONDS OF CHRISTMAS COLLAGE MUSIC, THEN IT UNDERSCORES CAPTAIN HULSE WRITING A LETTER TO HIS MOTHER ON DECEMBER 26, 1914.

CAPTAIN HULSE
My Dearest Mother, Just returned to billets after the most extraordinary Christmas in the trenches you could possibly imagine.
Words fail me completely in trying to describe it, but here it goes.
The Germans began by placing candles on their trenches and on trees, then continued the celebration by singing more Christmas carols.
Our men responded by singing carols of their own.
The two sides continued by shouting Christmas greetings to each other. Soon thereafter, there were excursions across No Man's Land, where small gifts were exchanged, such as food, tobacco and alcohol, and souvenirs such as buttons and hats.
By midnight, as Christmas Eve turned to Christmas Day, we all spontaneously sang Auld Lang Syne in this open field.
It was all a cacophonous mix of English, Scots, Irish, Prussians, Austrians, all joining in. It was absolutely astounding, and if I had not been there I would never believe the events of that night. On Christmas Day, the artillery in the region stayed silent.
The truce also allowed a breathing spell where recently killed soldiers could be brought back behind their lines by burial parties.
Joint services were held, each attended by soldiers from both sides. During one of the services, I spotted a German officer, some sort of lieutenant I should think, and being a bit of a collector as you know, I intimated to him that I had taken a fancy to some of his buttons.

He nodded, yes. I brought out my wire clippers and, with a few deft snips, removed a couple of his buttons and put them in my pocket. I then gave him two of mine in exchange.

One of the most telling events occurred when one of my machine gunners, who was a bit of an amateur hairdresser in civil life, started cutting the unnaturally long hair of a young Boche lad, who was patiently kneeling on the ground whilst the automatic clippers crept up the back of his neck.

I can truly say, these last two days have been the most memorable in my life.

I wouldn't have missed this weird and unique Christmas for anything. Unfortunately, on this day December 26, 1914, the hardened reality of war has returned.

General Sir Horace Smith-Dorrien, commander of the British II Corps, has issued orders forbidding any further friendly communication with the opposing German troops.

Artillery bombardment is to commence within the hour.

I love you and miss home beyond your imagining.

Your devoted son, Edward.

COLLAGE OF MUSIC FOR 10 SECONDS, SEGUEING TO UNDERSCORE

ROSA MAYREDER

I write to you, my sister in peace and in mourning for the 16 million souls who now journey through the oblivion of darkness that was imposed upon them by the belligerent men of this world.

On this day, December 24, 1918, where are the young men who should be stomping through our home with shouts of Christmas joy? There are none. There are only old men who stare at the world with impotent rage, already planning for the slaughter of our future generations of youth.

I pray for your happiness, as I pray to regain my own.

– Your devoted friend, Rosa Mayreder

EMILY HOBHOUSE

My dearest Rosa. Your friendship and wisdom have been a constant comfort to me during the insanity of this conflict.

I do not have the gift of words to truly express the depth of my feelings. I would like to share a poem – a haunting lament for this wholesale sacrifice of our youth – from my friend, Margaret Postgate Cole.

The Falling Leaves
"Today, as I rode by, I saw the brown leaves dropping from their tree In a still afternoon, When no wind whirled them whistling to the sky, But thickly, silently, They fell, like snowflakes wiping out the noon; And wandered slowly thence For thinking of a gallant multitude Which now all withering lay, Slain by no wind of age or pestilence, But in their beauty strewed Like snowflakes falling on the Flemish clay."
I remain your devoted friend, Emily Hobhouse.

THE MUSICAL COLLAGE PLAYS FOR 10 SECONDS AND THEN UNDERSCORES THE CAST READING OF THE CREDITS.

ACTOR PORTRAYING (CAPTAIN HULSE)

The Christmas Eve Truce was written by Julio Martinez. The characters in this drama are based on actual people. **Emily Hobhouse** - born April 9, 1860 - was a British welfare campaigner, and avid opponent of the First World War. She organized the writing, signing and publishing of the "Open Christmas Letter," addressed "To the Women of Germany and Austria." Through her efforts, thousands of women and children were fed daily for more than a year in central Europe after this war. She is portrayed by (fill in name).

ACTRESS PLAYING (EMILY HOBHOUSE)

Bruce Bairnsfather joined the Royal Warwickshire Regiment in 1914 and served with a machine gun unit in France until 1915, when he was hospitalized with shell shock and hearing damage.

Bruce, a talented artist, developed a humorous cartoon series for the British Bystander about life in the trenches, featuring "Old Bill", a curmudgeonly Scottish soldier. Bruce is portrayed by (fill in name) and Bill is brought to life by (fill in name).

ACTOR PLAYING BRUCE BAIRNSFATHER)

Rosa Mayreder, born in Vienna in 1858, was a noted Austrian author, painter, musician and feminist, and wrote many articles and books criticizing European society's double standard discrimination against women. During the First World War, Rosa engaged in the peace movement and later became the chairman of the International Women's League for Peace and Liberty. She is portrayed by (fill in name).

ACTRESS PLAYING ROSA MAYREDER

The character of **Corporal Phillip Frings** is culled from the letters of Captain Hulse, in which he wrote of a German soldier, a translator, who entered the battlefield, pleading with the British command to allow his countrymen to observe Christmas Eve on their side of the battle lines. He is portrayed by (fill in name).

ACTOR PORTRAYING CORPORAL FRINGS

Captain Sir Edward Hulse was born in 1889, educated at Eton and Oxford. In 1913, he received his commission and was assigned his first battlefield command in August of the next year. Captain Hulse was killed at Neuve Chapelle on March 12th, 1915. A tablet recording the manner of his death was put up to his memory in Salisbury Cathedral by the citizens of the town. He is portrayed by (fill in name).

ACTOR PORTRAYING BILL

We wish you all a blessed and peaceful holiday season.

CLOSING MUSIC The End

ALL IS CALM, ALL IS BRIGHT

(THE STORY OF 'SILENT NIGHT')

A Radio Play
by Julio Martinez

Narrator –Ageless Sage
Franz Gruber – Musician/choir master
Fr. Joseph Mohr – a young pastor
Mrs. Maria Gruber – Franz's wife
Peter & Anna – two teenage singers in the choir
Bitta – The Gruber's five-year-old daughter

NARRATOR
It is a fact that in 1818, on Christmas Eve, a simple, hastily composed tribute to the birth of the Christ child was performed for the first time at Midnight Mass in St. Nicholas Church in the village of Oberndorf, Austria. On that night, a song was born that eventually would make its way into the hearts of people throughout the world. Now translated into hundreds of languages, it is sung by untold millions every December from small chapels in the Andes and Appalachia to soaring cathedrals in all the great cities of the world. And like many wondrous events, the story of its creation is quite simple…as simple as young people in love…a

family of field mice in search of a home…or the desire to serve dinner on time.

MARIA GRUBER
Herr Gruber…Herr Gruber. Where are you?

BITTA
Where's Poppa?

NARRATOR
Meal time was certainly on the mind of Frau Maria Gruber when she marched briskly with her young daughter into the sanctuary of St. Nicholas Church at noon on Christmas Eve, in search of her not always punctual husband, Franz Xavier Gruber, the church's choirmaster, who, at that moment, just happened to be lodged deep within the inner workings of the sanctuary's immense pipe organ.

MARIA GRUBER
Herr Gruber. Your dinner is absolutely cold…cold and ruined. Herr Gruber!

FRANZ GRUBER (from a distance)
I can't really come to dinner at the moment, my dear. I am sort of…stuck.

BITTA
Poppa's a ghost.

MARIA GRUBER
Bita, shush! (TO FRANZ) Stuck indeed. Come out here this instant. Where are you?

PETER
Herr Gruber is inside the organ, Frau Gruber.

MARIA GRUBER

Oh! Peter, Anna. You're here too?
What do you mean my husband is <u>inside</u> the organ.

BITTA

The organ ate Poppa?

ANNA

No. He's trying to fix it.

PETER

Anna and I have been up in the choir loft waiting to rehearse our solos for tonight's Midnight Mass.

ANNA

But the organ won't make a sound and Herr Gruber is fixing it.

FRANZ GRUBER

Was fixing it. I think the situation may be hopeless.

PETER

You mean there won't be any music for Christmas Eve Mass.

ANNA

Oh no! That would be terrible.

PETER

And this is my last mass before I leave.

MARIA GRUBER.

Peter? Where are you going?

ANNA

He is going to Salzburg to study for his university entrance exams…even though he doesn't have to go.

PETER

Anna, you know I can't get the tutoring help I need here in Oberndorf to pass my exams. I am not as smart as you. I do need to go to Salzburg.

FRANZ GRUBER

When do you leave, Peter?

PETER

In one week, right after the New Year. Both my mother and father are already in Salzburg arranging for my accommodations. So, this is my last opportunity to sing at our church.

MARIA GRUBER.

Herr Gruber, What is wrong with the organ? And how did you get stuck in it?

FRANZ GRUBER

I tried to wedge myself between the grand E pipe and the E flat pipe and I got temporarily wedged. The pipes are fine. I am fine.

MARIA GRUBER

And why won't the organ play?

FRANZ GRUBER

I can answer that in one word…mice!

BITTA

Mice?

MARIA GRUBER

Mice! What do you mean, mice?

MR. GRUBER

A family of field mice has made a home for themselves within our church's organ. And in the process, have chewed their way through the organ's bellows. No bellows, no air. No air, no sound. No sound, no music for Midnight Mass.

ANNA

Is there any way to fix it before tonight's Mass?

FRANZ GRUBER

I have sent for the tailor, Herr Frings. If we can put a temporary patch on the bellows, we should be able to get through tonight's service. We'll work right up to the start of Mass if we have to.

MARIA GRUBER

Oh no you won't work here in the sanctuary right up to Mass. You will be home for supper at six. Did you forget that we have a guest coming to dinner?

FRANZ GRUBER

Who?

MARIA GRUBER

Herr Gruber, I cannot believe you sometimes. Father Joseph Mohr, our new assistant pastor arrived in Oberndorf today. And we are welcoming him as our guest for supper tonight before services begin.

FRANZ GRUBER

Some welcome. Father Mohr is going to preside over his first service at Christmas Eve Midnight Mass tonight in a church with no organ and no music… unless Herr Frings and I can patch the hole in the bellows.

MARIA GRUBER

You do what you can. But I want you home to greet our new pastor no later than 6 o clock…Sharp! Do you understand me Herr Gruber.

FRANZ GRUBER

I understand you and I can hear you quite well, Frau Gruber.

MARIA GRUBER

Peter, since your parents are already in Salzburg, you will dine with us tonight. I insist.

PETER

Thank you, Frau Gruber…if it is no trouble.

MARIA GRUBER

Making sure my family and friends are properly fed is never any trouble. Anna, would you care to join us as well?

ANNA

I'm sure my parents won't mind. I would love to join you and meet the new pastor, if you have room.

MARIA GRUBER

Of course we have room. Herr Gruber! Six o'clock sharp! Come along, Bitta.

BITTA

Can we keep the mice, Momma?

NARRATOR

So Frau Gruber left her husband to his labors and returned to her kitchen to prepare supper. Peter and Anna rushed to her home in the village to petition for Anna to be allowed to attend Christmas Eve supper with the choirmaster and his wife.

SOUNDS OF WALKING RAPIDLY THOUGH THE SNOW.

PETER

Anna, why are you walking so fast?

ANNA

It's a busy day, Peter.
Dinner with Herr Gruber's family.
Sing at Midnight Mass.
And then bid you goodbye...
Even though you....

PETER

Anna, please listen to me.
If I am ever to have a life her in Oberndorf,
I must complete my studies at University.

ANNA

What are you talking about?
Oberndorf is your home.

PETER

Anna, if I am not admitted in University,
My father insists I must join the military.

ANNA

What?

PETER

Anna, you know my father was a career soldier.
He fought against Napoleon at Waterloo
He is constantly fearing that Napoleon will come back and invade Austria. He did it before.

ANNA

But Peter. Napoleon is imprisoned or in exile on some island in the Atlantic Ocean.

PETER

Well, father claims that Napoleon escaped from an island before and within weeks raised an army of over 200,000.
Our country put a bounty on his head. Father claims that Napoleon will come back and attack us.

ANNA

Oh Peter, you are not like your father. You are not a soldier. You are an artist and a scholar. And such a beautiful singer.

PETER

I sing in the choir because you are there. And my pitiful efforts at scholarship have only been successful with the help of you and my mother. Anna, I am scared. I don't want to leave. I don't want to leave you.

ANNA

Peter, then go to Salzburg and prepare for you entrance exams. Take excellent notes. You will have two days after your preparatory studies before the actual exams and I will coach you. You will get into University.

PETER

Anna, you will do this for me?

ANNA

Oh Peter....Don't you know? I would do anything for you.

NARRATOR

As Peter and Anna continue on to Anna's home, Frau Gruber is busily preparing the Christmas Eve feast, while keeping a watchful eye on her ever-inquisitive daughter, Bitta.

BITTA

What you making, Momma?

FRAU GRUBER

Schnitzel! Now, I need three bowls, Here's two. Where's the third. Ah here we are.

BITTA

Why three, Momma?

FRAU GRUBER

The first is for flour; the second is for the eggs; and the third is filled with bread crumbs.

BITTA

I like Schnitzel.

FRAU GRUBER

That's good. You are Austrian. Schnitzel is hearty. It is a staple. Do you remember what I told you about *Gründlichkeit?* It is how we live our lives...with rules. Cooking a veal cutlet is a lesson in cooking with precision.

No Bitta, please. I need to concentrate.
The cutlets are dipped into each bowl like this.

BITTA

Can I do one?

FRAU GRUBER

Yes. Now, you stand in front of me on the bench, so you can reach. The veal cutlets are on the plate on the left.
You just take one and go from bowl to bowl to bowl.

BITTA

Like this?

FRAU GRUBER

Yes, that's fine. Make sure your cutlet has an even amount from each bowl, so that it cooks evenly. Good girl.

BITTA

This is fun.

FRAU GRUBER

It will be fun. If everything is finished on time and your father is not late for supper. Now the cutlets need to be fried in butter and then served with a garnish of lemons, anchovy and capers, plus a sprig of parsley. And this has to be timed with the roasting of the potatoes, with everything finishing together.

BITTA

We can do that.

FRAU GRUBER

Yes, Bitta. We can do that.

NARRATOR

While Frau Gruber and daughter continued with their labors in the kitchen, a young, nervous new assistant pastor, Father Joseph Mohr, was sitting in his room reading over a decidedly homesick letter he had just penned to his grandfather in his native village of Mariapfarr.

FR. JOSEPH MOHR

"...and in conclusion, grandfather, please tell everyone in the congregation how much I miss being with them this Christmas Eve. Tonight, I must give a sermon in a brand new church. I pray I do justice to this honor. Oh, and thank you for sending my papers and sermons ahead. They were waiting for me when I arrived. I didn't expect you to send everything that was in my desk. You even sent my humble poems. I had forgotten about them. One in particular, I just might try to work into this evening's sermon. I will end this now. I have been invited to the choirmaster's home for supper before the services begin. I hope I make a good impression. Your loving grandson, Joseph."

NARRATOR

That evening, Father Joseph Mohr was quite punctual arriving at the Gruber home,. As were Anna and Peter.

MRS. GRUBER

And where is Herr Gruber?

PETER

I'm sure the time just got away from him. I'll go fetch him.

ANNA

I'll go along, too.

FRANZ GRUBER

No fetching necessary. I am home, safe and sound but, sad to say, not victorious.

MARIA GRUBER

Oh Herr Gruber, the organ can't be fixed?

PETER

There won't be any music?

ANNA

On Christmas Eve?

BITTA

Where are the mice?

FR. JOSEPH MOHR

Am I to understand that the church's organ is broken?

MARIA GRUBER

Oh, forgive me my manners. Herr Gruber, tonight we have the honor of entertaining Father Joseph Mohr, the new assistant pastor of St. Nicholas Church. Father Mohr, my husband and your choirmaster, Herr Franz Gruber.

FR. JOSEPH MOHR

It is an honor to meet your sir.

FRANZ GRUBER

The honor is mine, Father Mohr. I just wish we could honor your first service at our church with music;

but no amount of patching will support the organ's bellows. The mice have won the day.

FR. JOSEPH MOHR

What music were you planning for this evening?

FRANZ GRUBER

Two interludes from Cantata 142 by Johan Sebastion Bach.

FR. JOSEPH MOHR

Ah yes, the Christmas Cantata.

PETER

Anna and I were each going to perform solos.

ANNA

And this is the last time Peter will be performing at our church before he leaves for Salzburg.

FRANZ GRUBER

But we cannot perform a Bach cantata or any other cantata without an organ. It would sound absurd.

MRS. GRUBER

Herr Gruber. Supper is ready.

BITTA

Time to eat.

FR. JOSEPH MOHR

Herr Gruber. At my previous church, I conducted the youth classes. Perhaps, if you have some simpler Christmas music, I could accompany Peter or Anna on my guitar, after I give my sermon.

FRANZ GRUBER

I don't have anything that would be appropriate for guitar accompaniment. I would literally have to compose something with a simple melody and simple chords, but I have no text.

MARIA GRUBER

Mr. Gruber, supper is getting cold.

BITTA

Time to eat.

FR. JOSEPH MOHR

Herr Gruber, I have a poem that I was perhaps going to incorporate into my sermon, but I think it would lend itself to a melody quite well.

ANNA

Oh, Peter and I are quick studies. Herr Gruber, perhaps you could arrange it as a duet.

FRANZ GRUBER

We can certainly try. Father Mohr, Anna, Peter, we'll go to my study and…

MRS. GRUBER

Herr Gruber, honored guest Father Mohr, Anna and Peter. None of you are going anywhere until you have sat at my table, offered grace to our bountiful Lord and partaken of my humble supper, which I have toiled over all day. Then you can go off and make all the music you want.

BITTA

Time to eat.

NARRATOR

At St. Thomas, as in most Austrian and German village churches, Midnight Mass actually began about 11 pm. At the completion of Frau Gruber's quite excellent Christmas Eve Supper, Franz Gruber, Anna and Peter did indeed retreat to the choirmaster's study with the pastor's poem, while the author dashed back the rectory to retrieve his guitar.

FRANZ GRUBER

That is an excellent looking instrument you have, Father Mohr.

FR. JOSEPH MOHR

Yes, it was built for me in Vienna. It was a gift from my grandfather when I completed my seminary studies.

FRANZ GRUBER

Would you mind playing something for me, so I have some idea of you technique on the instrument.

FR. JOSEPH MOHR

Certainly. This is from the first Cellos Suite in G by Johann Back. It has been adapted for the guitar.

PLAY: CELLO SUITE IN G BY JOHAN SEBASTIAN BACH (2:23)

FRANZ GRUBER

That was excellent, Father Mohr. You are a fine musician.

FR. JOSEPH MOHR

Thank you, sir.

FRANZ GRUBER

I especially like the way Bach frames the piece with arpeggios. That style lends itself quite well for an accompaniment for singing.

ANNA

I am excited to do this.

PETER

Me too.

FRANZ GRUBER

Excellent. Now Father Mohr, let's look at your poem and work this out.

NARRATOR

Within an hour, Franz Gruber had outlined the melody and had begun to teach it to Anna and Peter. He then sketched a chord accompaniment for Father Mohr.

FATHER MOHR

Why this is quite easy to play. There are only three chords.

NARRATOR

Christmas Eve Midnight Mass began right at 11pm. The blessings were offered. Communion was observed. As the new assistant pastor, Father Joseph Mohr offered a sermon that displayed a boyish enthusiasm for his calling. At the conclusion, he moved from the pulpit to a small chair that had been placed directly in front of the congregation pews where his guitar was placed. Anna and Peter stood at either side of Father Mohr. With nothing more to do, a clearly nervous Franz Gruber sat with his wife in the front pew.

MARIA GRUBER

Will it be all right, Herr Gruber?

FRANZ GRUBER

Frau Gruber, it is a simple Christmas carol with a simple message. I'm sure no one will remember it after this evening. But I think it is quite suitable.

THE SINGING OF SILENT NIGHT BY ANNA AND PETER, TWO CHORUSES.

PETER & ANNA
(sung)

Silent night, holy night,
All is calm, all is bright
Round yon virgin mother and Child.
Holy Infant, so tender and mild,
Sleep in heavenly peace,
Sleep in heavenly peace.
Silent night, holy night,
Shepherds quake at the sight;
Glories stream from heaven afar,
Heavenly hosts sing Alleluia!
Christ the Savior is born,
Christ the Savior is born!

INSTRUMENTAL OF 'SILENT NIGHT' UNDERSCORES THE NARRATOR

NARRATOR

Indeed. *Silent Night*, composed so quickly on Christmas Eve, has proven quite suitable; in fact, suitable enough to become the most beloved and most performed Christmas Carols in history.

PETER & ANNA
(sung)

"sleep in heavenly peace,
sleep I heavenly peace."

BITTA
(SUNG) "Sleep in heavenly peace."

THE END

ONE HORSE OPEN SLEIGH

(THE STORY OF "JINGLE BELLS")

By Julio Martinez

Eliza Pierpont, late 20s
James Pierpont, early 30s
Rev John Pierpont, mid-30s
Fanny Bright, early 30s
George Kimebaly, late 30s

INTRO MUSIC:

ELIZA PIERPONT

I have been asked to say a few words about my late husband, James Lord Pierpont.

He would have been so proud to see you fine folks of Savannah gathered here today. Indeed, he was a wonderful musician and composer.

But I must say, back in 1857 he would have been most surprised that you would be honoring him for a little tune he wrote to be nothing more than a minstrel drinking ditty, never suspecting it would become such a popular Christmastime song.

SONG: 'RING THE BELL, FANNIE' CASUALLY BEING SUNG BY JAMES L PIERPONT AS HE IS PREPARING TO LEAVE THE HOUSE OF HIS BROTHER, REV. JOHN

PIERPONT, THE MINISTER OF SAVANNAH, GEORGIA UNITARIAN CHURCH.

REV JOHN PIERPONT
James, where are you going?

JAMES PIERPONT
Out!

REV JOHN
Out. But what about the music for services?

JAMES
Services are on Sunday. This is Thursday. I'll have the music arranged for the chorus tomorrow. Tonight, I am meeting George Kimebaly.

REV JOHN
Kimebaly? That minstrel man. James, I thought you were done with that minstrel show nonsense. You are now the music director of Savannah Unitarian Church.
You're engaged to the daughter of Savannah's mayor.

JAMES
So? You're the church's minister and you write secular poetry.
I write church music and I love writing show tunes.
I'm doing a new set of songs for Campbell's Minstrels.
George is their new manager. I'm meeting him at the Tavern.

REV JOHN
Campbell's Minstrels? Isn't that a Northern group?

JAMES
Campbell's Minstrels is the biggest show group in New York, next to the Christy Minstrels. And George wants me to write four new songs for them.
I'm....John, why are you frowning?

REV JOHN

I don't think this is the time to be seen in taverns with show people from the North. Savannah is very conservative in its thinking...

JAMES

Brother, I know about your problems with members of the congregation. And I know the Mayor has been to see you about this.

REV JOHN

They don't want me to continue to advocate for Abolition.

JAMES

I know.

REV JOHN

You and I were raised in the North, James.
But I am trying to get the congregation to understand that Abolition is not an issue of the Northern States.
It is a human issue.

JAMES

And you think me sharing a pint in a Savannah tavern is going to inflame the masses?

REV JOHN

It is 1857 and it is already obvious that Abolition is going to be a major issue in the 1860 election. I would just like to deal with this as the Pastor of a Southern Church who is not being influenced by Northern liberals.

JAMES

John, George Kimebaly is a minstrel. All he wants to do is drink and sing.

MUSIC OF A GUITAR & BANJO & THS SOUNDS OF A CROWD HAVING A GREAT TIME ENJOYING THEMSELVES AT SAVANNAH TAVERN. OUT OF THIS DIN CAN BE HEARD THE VOICES OF GEORGE KIMEBALY AND FANNIE BRIGHT.

FANNY

Well to quote Shakespeare, everyone is certainly "well met" here.

GEORGE

Fanny, my dear. We are through with The Bard. This is the 19h century and Minstrel shows are sweeping the country. And we are going sweep right along with them.

FANNY

The Christy Minstrels have New York all to themselves. How you gonna beat them?

GEORGE

With new music, my dear. And I have one of the best composers in America who is going to create a new show for my Campbell's Troupe....he just doesn't know it, yet.

FANNY

Oh, you are up to something. Who is it?

GEORGE

An old friend of yours from Medford, Massachusetts, James Lord Pierpont

FANNY

Jimmy? Oh no you don't. Jimmy, I mean James and I are old friends but that's it.
I haven't seen him in years.

GEORGE

Well old friends, should not be forgot. In fact, here he is now. (SHOUTNG) James! James! Over here, at the bar.

DIN OF THE CROWD LESSENS AS JAMES PPROACHES THE BAR.

JAMES

George, glad to see you. How long....Fanny?

FANNY

James? It's good to see you, Jimmy. It has been too long.

JAMES

You're looking great. So, how do you two know each other?

FANNY

We worked a season together with Booth's Shakespeare Company at the Winter Garden in New York. Then two years ago I got a job as choir director for the Gardner School for Girls in Manhattan and I quit performing.

GEORGE

Not for long. I read she was touring with her Gardner School choir, appearing here in Savannah this weekend. It's meant to be.

JAMES

What's meant to be?

GEORGE

A new Broadway show, starring Fanny and me, and Campbell's Minstrels, with all new songs by James Lord Pierpont.

JAMES

I agreed to write four songs, not a whole show.

And besides, women do not appear in Minstrel Shows.

FANNY
That's what I told him.

GEORGE
It's 1857. It's a brand new age.
This won't be a typical minstrel show.
It will have a plot and characters.
The Minstrels will be like chorus members.

THE GUITAR AND BANJO PLAYING IN THE BACKGROUND HAVE SEGUED INTO A POPULAR BAR TUNE, 'NOTTINGHAM ALE.'

GEORGE
Fanny, you know this song. We sang it in "A Midummer's Nights Dream."
Do it with me. Let's inspire our old pal, James.
(TO THE BAND) Boys, over here.

FANNIE
I don' know.

GEORGE
Oh, come on.

GEORGE (singing)
"When Venus, the goddess of beauty and love
Arose from the froth that swam on the sea."

FANNY (singing)
"Minerva sprang out of the cranium of Jove
A coy, sullen dame as most mortals agree."

GEORGE

"But Bacchus, they tell us, that prince of good fellows
Was Jupiter's son, pray attend my tale
They who thus chatter mistake quite the matter
He sprang from a barrel of Nottingham Ale."

GEORGE & FANNY

"Nottingham Ale, me boys, Nottingham Ale
No liquor on earth is like Nottingham Ale
Nottingham Ale, me boys, Nottingham Ale
No liquor on earth is like Nottingham Ale."

GEORGE

"You bishops and curates, priests, deacons and vicars
When once you have tasted, you all must agree
That Nottingham Ale is the best of all liquors
And none understands a good creature like thee."

FANNY

"It dispels every vapor, saves pen, ink and paper
For when you've a mind in your pulpit to rail
It'll open your throats, you may preach without notes
When inspired with a bumper of Nottingham Ale."

GEORGE & FANNY

"Nottingham Ale, me boys, Nottingham Ale
No liquor on earth is like Nottingham Ale
Nottingham Ale, me boys, Nottingham Ale
No liquor on earth is like Nottingham Ale."

SOUND OF THE DIN WITH APPLAUSE FROM THE CROWD.

GEORGE

Thank you all. Thank you.

JAMES

You performed that in a Shakespeare play?

GEORGE

It's a whole new world in New York, my boy.
I played one of the Mechanicals. Bottom!

FANNY

And I was one of Tatiana's fairy maidens.

GEORGE

We sang these popular songs throughout the play.
It was a big hit.
The time is right my boy.
Broadway is ready for new ideas.

JAMES

My barnstorming year are over, George.

GEORGE

That's right. Fanny, James is now the music director and organist for a Savannah church.

FANNY

Impressive.

GEORGE

And engaged to be married to the daughter of the Mayor of Savannah.

FANNY

Oh....very impressive.

JAMES

George, I can write a few songs for you, but like I said, I cannot take the time to write a whole show.

GEORGE

I don't get you. Here you are, a pillar of the Savannah community.
Yet, you have written popular songs for Kunkle's Nightingale Opera Troupe.
You have already written a song for Campbell's Minstrels.
You have collaborated with the lyricist Marshall S. Pike.
And you have written songs published by Miller and Beacham in Baltimore and by Oliver Ditson and Company New York.
James you are a songwriter. Admit it.

JAMES

Yes, I love writing songs and I will keep doing it. But my life has changed.
I am 35 years old. I've had my adventures.
In 1932, I ran away from boarding school to board a whaling ship called the Shark.
Then I served in the US Navy until I was 21.
I tried to settle down after that. I moved to Medford. I got married.

GEORGE

I didn't know that.

FANNY

To Millicent Cowee. She and I were friends and we sang together.

GEORGE

Fanny, you sang in church?

FANNY

No. Medford had a community choir. James was the director.
James did all the arranging and even wrote some songs for us.
We did quite well.

GEORGE

You mean you did quite well.

Edwin Booth saw you and plucked you right out to join his troupe.

FANNY

And Millicent stayed and married James.

GEORGE

So, any of the choir songs we can use in our show.

JAMES

Don't get ahead of yourself, George.
Things did not work out for me in Medford.
In 1849, when gold was discovered in California,
I left my wife to open a business in San Francisco.
Millicent went to live with my father.
My business failed when a fire destroyed all my goods.

FANNY

I didn't know that, Jimmy.

GEORGE

So what did you do?

JAMES

I worked a bit as photographer. And I wrote some songs for shows.
Then last year, my brother John accepted this post as
Pastor of Savannah Unitarian Church and asked me to join him.
On my way home, I received news that Millicent had died.

FANNY

I heard. I am so sorry.

JAMES

Thank you. So, I am here. Now, I am newly engaged to be married.

GEORGE

So, you don't want to write the songs for my new show.

Julio Martinez

JAMES

I didn't say that.

GEORGE

Ahha. When can we start?

JAMES

Don't get ahead of yourself.
I have to work things out at the Church.
And right now, my head isn't into writing popular songs.

FANNY

I know one you have already written, "Wake Lady Wake."

JAMES

You remember that?

GEORGE

I wanna hear it.

JAMES

It's duet I wrote for Millicent and Fanny to sing with the Medford Chorus.

FANNY

And I played the guitar.

(TO UNSEEN MUSICIAN)
Sir, may borrow your instrument?
Thank you.

(SOUND OF GUITAR INTRO TO THE SONG)

Come on Jimmy, sing it with me. You start.
SONG: "Wake Lady Wake"

JAMES
"Soft zephyrs flow o'er all below,
Stars sprinkle brightly, love let us go.
Sweet balmy airs, whisper of love.
So wake my lady, look down from above."

FANNY
"Sleeping yet, thy heart will go free,
So wake my lady and listen to me.
Sleeping yet, they heart will go free,

JAMES AND FANNY
So wake my lady and listen to me."

JAMES
"Wake Lady Wake, love bid thee rise.
Come view the stars bright studing the skies.
Bold may thy heart beat love for me,
Life is worth nothing if loved not by thee."

FANNY
"Sleeping yet, thy heart will go free,
So wake my lady and listen to me.
Sleeping yet, they heart will go free,

JAMES AND FANNY
So wake my lady and listen to me."

SONG ENDS WITH APPLAUSE FROM THE CROWD

GEORGE
We've got our first song for the new show.
What's next?

JAMES

What's next is me returning to the church rectory tomorrow and arranging four hymns for the chorus, then rehearse them for Sunday's service.

GEORGE

OK, OK. But at least think about songs for the show.
I want these to be new and so different the whole town will be talking about them.

FANNY

Oh, write a song about the time you gave me a ride home in your sleigh. That had the whole town of Medford talking.

GEORGE

What? What?

JAMES

We got into an accident.

FANNY

I'll say.

GEORGE

Tell me.

FANNY

Well, the Medford Chorus was rehearsing in the reception room at the City Hall building, which was right in the middle of town.
When the rehearsal was over, James kept Millicent and me to rehearse our solos and our duet.
He kept us there for an hour.

JAMES

It was in December and it had snowed most of the day, but the streets had been swept clean.

FANNY

But during the time, James was rehearsing Millicent and me, it snowed again.
The roads were covered and I lived on the other side of town.

GEORGE

What did you do?

JAMES

Millicent insisted I take Fanny home in my sleigh.

FANNY

His one horse sleigh, with only two seats.

GEORGE

How scandalous.

JAMES

That's what I told Millicent, but she insisted.

GEORGE

So, what happened?

JAMES

Well, we were about half way to Fanny's house when I approached a corner that had a huge tree blocking my view of the road.

FANNY

A milk wagon came right in our path.

JAMES

My horse reared up and turned sharply.

FANNY

And tossed us both out of the sleigh, into a snowdrift.

JAMES

Barrels from the milk wagon tumbled onto the street.
The wagon driver was yelling a lot.

GEORGE

Didn't you hear the wagon?

JAMES

In that snow, you couldn't hear anything while in the sleigh.
But after our accident, you certainly could hear the milk wagon driver yelling.
It seemed like the whole town came running out of their houses.
They thought we were hurt.

FANNY

We were fine.
But we did make the town's newspaper.

GEORGE

The newspaper?

JAMES

Those smaller, open sleighs had become quite popular up north.
And there had been a few mishaps, especially driving at night.

FANNY

The newspaper report noted that James couldn't hear or see the milk wagon at the intersection.

JAMES

So, there was an editorial in the newspaper demanding that all sleighs operating in the town of Medford have small bells attached to the horse's bridle so you could hear them coming.

GEORGE

So what happened?

JAMES

The Medford City Council voted on it at the next meeting.

FANNY

And it passed.

JAMES

And now I must be off.
I will think about your songs this weekend.

THE MUSIC IN THR BACKGROUND BEGINS TO PLAY 'LUBLY FAN' (BUFFALO GALS)

GEORGE

Then be off.
I will escort Fanny back to her hotel.
After one last song. Now this is a Minstrel Song that is popular all over.
Give us one like this.

(SUNG)
"As I was lumb'ring down de street,
Down de street, down de street;
A pretty girl I chanc'd to meet,
O she was fair to view."

GEORGE AND FANNY

"Den lubly Fan will you come out tonight,
Will you come out to night, will you come out tonight;
Den lubly Fan will you come out to night,
An' dance by de lite ob de moon."

Julio Martinez

THE CHOIR REHEARAL ROOM AT SAVANNAH UNITARIAN CHURCH, SATURDAY MORNING

ELIZA
Still a work, James.

JAMES
Well, I finished arranging the hymns for the choir.
We rehearsed them yesterday afternoon.

ELIZA
So, what are you working on?

JAMES
I promised an old friend I would write some songs for his show.
I had some ideas and was just jotting them down.

ELIZA
Would these songs also be appropriate to sing at our wedding?

JAMES
Ah, no. They wouldn't.
They are for a Minstrel Show.

ELIZA
A Minstrel show in Savannah?

JAMES
No, Eliza. It is for Campbell's Minstrels in New York.

ELIZA
I see. Well if you are going to take time to go to New York,
Then maybe we should delay our wedding.

JAMES
Eliza, there is no need to delay our wedding.

I am not going to New York.
I have thought about this. I am writing four songs which I can do here.
I am not going anywhere.
Someone else can write the score for this show.
I will never leave my wife alone, again.

ELIZA

James, I have heard the talk.
If your brother John continues to advocate for Abolition,
The town may close down his pulpit.

JAMES

Is that what your father says?

ELIZA

That's what everyone is saying.

JAMES

Well, my darling. You direct the church's children's choir,
We may be both looking for new jobs.

ELIZA

Here in Savannah?

JAMES

Yes, here in Savannah.

ENTRACT MUSIC OF 'WAIT FOR THE WAGON'
A REHEARSAL ROOM IN NEW YORK CITY

FANNY

So, when were you married?

JAMES

Two days ago. I owed you these tunes so we decided to spend our honeymoon in New York.

GEORGE

So, how long are you here for?

JAMES

Just this weekend. Eliza and I have to head back on Monday.

GEORGE

Well, the songs are great.

FANNY

Especially this one, "One Horse Open Sleigh" (SOUND OF SHEET MUSIC)
I am flattered that you are immortalizing me in song.

JAMES

Well, you were there.

GEORGE

And since this is probably the last time the three of us will be performing together, Lets give it a go.

PIANO INTRO

GEORGE

"Dashing thro' the snow,
In a one-horse open sleigh,
O'er the hills we go,
Laughing all the way;"

FANNY

"Bells on bob tail ring,
Making spirits bright,
Oh what sport to ride and sing
A sleighing song to night."

JAMES, GEORGE & FANNY

"Jingle bells, Jingle bells,
Jingle all the way;
Oh! what joy it is to ride
In a one horse open sleigh.
Jingle bells, Jingle bells,
Jingle all the way;
Oh! what joy it is to ride
In a one horse open sleigh."

JAMES

"A day or two ago,
I thought I'd take a ride,
And soon Miss Fannie Bright
Was seated by my side,"

FANNY

"The horse was lean and lank;
Misfortune seemed his lot,
He got into a drifted bank,
And we, we got upsot."

JAMES, GEORGE & FANNY

"Jingle bells, Jingle bells,
Jingle all the way;
Oh! what joy it is to ride
In a one horse open sleigh.
Jingle bells, Jingle bells,
Jingle all the way;
Oh! what joy it is to ride
In a one horse open sleigh."

FANNY

"Now the ground is white
Go it while you're young,"

GEORGE
"Take the girls tonight and sing this sleighing song;"

JAMES
"Just get a bobtailed bay
Two forty as his speed[b]
Hitch him to an open sleigh
And crack! you'll take the lead."

JAMES, GEORGE & FANNY
"Jingle bells, Jingle bells,
Jingle all the way;
Oh! what joy it is to ride
In a one horse open sleigh.
Jingle bells, Jingle bells,
Jingle all the way;
Oh! what joy it is to ride
In a one horse open sleigh."

ENTRACTE INSTRUMENTAL OF 'ONE HORSE OPEN SLEIGH'

ELIZA
When James and I returned to Savannah from New York, there was more talk of the problems between the North and the South. James's brother John was facing a crisis.

JOHN
James, the City Council is going to vote in the Spring.
I believe they are going to close us down.

JAMES
But why? Your sermons have been wonderful.
You have spoken eloquently....

The Eight Plays of Christmas

JOHN

No one is listening. James, I am going to stay in my ministry here in Savannah until I am displaced. When that happens, I will return to Massachusetts and continue my work.
What are you going to do, James?

JAMES

I am married and we are expecting a child.
I will stay with my wife and family here in Savannah.
John, once we get through with the Presidential elections,
Everything will calm down again. You'll see.

JOHN

Not everything is as simple as your songs, my brother.
But perhaps you are right.

ENTREACTE MUSIC

ELIZA

The year 1859 was very difficult. But we got through it.
The City Council did not close the church.
And as Christmas approached, James and I were actually optimistic.
I know all I was concerned about was getting the church's children's choir ready for its annual concert.

KNOCK ON DOOR

JAMES

Come in.

ELIZA

James, will you please help me with the recreation hall.
What are you reading?

JAMES

The New York Herald.
Campbell's Minstrels are going on tour.

ELIZA

Want to go with them?

JAMES

I am with them, at least my songs are.
They are still being performed.
And "One Horse Open Sleigh" is being published by Oliver Ditson.
I hear it is a popular song in the taverns.

ELIZA

Well that may be.
But as of right now, will you accompany me to the church rectory.

JAMES

Ah yes, the holiday decorations for the Children's Choir concert.
I will be happy to help. Lead the way.

ELIZA

Right this way, then.

ENTRACT MUSIC, SOUND OF DOOR OPENING

JAMES

Eliza, this looks splendid. You didn't need my help.
Oh, the children's chorus is still here.

ELIZA

Yes, there is one new number they are going to sing that I want you to hear.
(TO THE CHORUS) Natalie, Michael, I want you two to stand up front.

That's it one on either side of the chorus.

JAMES

Why are they holding bells?

ELIZA

You'll see. Everyone ready. Now one...two...one two

THE CHILDREN'S CHORUS

"Dashing thro' the snow,
In a one-horse open sleigh,
O'er the hills we go,
Laughing all the way;"
"Bells on bob tail ring,
Making spirits bright,
Oh what sport to ride and sing
A sleighing song to night."

Jingle bells, Jingle bells,
Jingle all the way;
Oh! what fun it is to ride
In a one horse open sleigh.
Jingle bells, Jingle bells,
Jingle all the way;
Oh! what fun it is to ride
In a one horse open sleigh."

"Dashing thro' the snow,
In a one-horse open sleigh,
O'er the hills we go,
Laughing all the way;"
"Bells on bob tail ring,
Making spirits bright,
Oh what sport to ride and sing

Julio Martinez

A sleighing song to night."

Jingle bells, Jingle bells,
Jingle all the way;
Oh! what fun it is to ride
In a one horse open sleigh.
Jingle bells, Jingle bells,
Jingle all the way;
Oh! what fun it is to ride
In a one horse open sleigh."

SOUND OF JAMES AND ELIZA APPLAUDING

JAMES

It sounds wonderful. Eliza, you changed the melody of the chorus section.

ELIZA

I hope you don't mind.
It was easier for the children to sing.
And they got so used to calling it, "Jingle Bells,"
that's the way it will be listed in the program.

JAMES

I don't mind. The song just sounds so different when children are singing it.

ELIZA

My husband, you may have set out to write a drinking song for a Minstrel show,
But what you have created is a joyful and wonderful Christmas song.
Merry Christmas, dear.

ENTREACT MUSIC LEADING TO THE PLAY'S CREDITS

ELIZA

Again, my husband would be so happy to see you all gathered here today, placing a plaque in his honor, celebrating his now much beloved composition of "Jingle Bells." The War of 1861 separated James from his family. The church closed. John returned to the North. We remained in Savannah, even if his nephew, the great John Pierpont Morgon, declared my husband "a great fool." It is my hope that his simple, yet joy-filled song will continue to be played as long as we celebrate this beautiful season. Thank you.

BING CROSBY, ANDREWS SISTERS VERSION SUNG DURING CLOSING CREDITS.

The End

CHRISTMAS IN TINSELTOWN

(THE STORY OF "WHITE CHRISTMAS")

A Radio Play by Julio Martinez

Cast
Mark Sandrich (producer/director, mid 30s)
Sandrich's secretary, Millie, mid 20s)
Irving Berlin (songwriter, mid 50s)
Martha Mears (singer/voiceover specialist, earls 30s)
Ken Carpenter (Kraft Music Hall Radio announcer/reporter, mid 30s)

'HURRAY FOR HOLLYWOOD' (BENNY GOODMAN VERSION, ONE CHORUS), SECOND CHORUS UNDERSCORES DIALOGUE, THE PARAMOUNT STUDIOS OFFICE OF PRODUCER/DIRECTOR MARK SANDRICH.

SANDRICH
Millie! Millie! Get in here.
Damn. Doesn't this thing work?
Millie!

SOUND OF DOOR OPENING

MILLIE
You yelled, Mr. Sandrich?

SANDRICH
Close the door.

SOUND OF DOOR CLOSING (MUSIC UNDERSCORE ENDS)

SANDRICH
Why didn't you answer the intercom?

MILLIE
I didn't need to.
I could have heard you all the way to the commissary.

SANDRICH
All right, now why don't you march back to your desk
and get Mr. Berlin on the phone for me.

MILLIE
I could phone Mr. Berlin but I won't get him.
Mr, Berlin and his wife left two hours ago for La Quinta.
They might even be checked in by now.

SANDRICH
Fine! Take a telegram. I want Irving to know how important our time schedule is?

MILLIE
I'll get my pad.

SANDRICH
Do you know if he took his piano?

MILLIE

I didn't ask. Now, what do you want me to send?

SANDRICH

O.K. May 7, 1940. Mr. Irving Berlin, C/O La Quinta Hotel, La Quinta, California.
Here goes, "Dear Irving, I have great news. STOP Paramount Studios wishes to purchase your story idea for a musical feature film, spotlighting a vacation hotel in Connecticut that is only open on the holidays. STOP We wish to contract you to compose the complete score, featuring at least a dozen new Irving Berlin songs. STOP Paramount is determined to have both Fred Astaire and Bing Crosby for this. STOP I will be directing <u>and</u> producing on this one. STOP What are you waiting for? Start composing.
DON'T STOP!

REPRISE OF 'HOORAY FOR HOLLYWOOD'

SANDRICH

What do you mean, the score isn't completed yet?
In January, you told me the score was almost finished.
That was three months ago.

BERLIN

The music for all the songs is finished and almost all of the lyrics.

SANDRICH

O.K. That's good.
We'll start casting in July.
Then we should be able to go into music rehearsals in August.
Location shooting in Sonoma begins December 1st.
That gives you a lot of time to finish the lyrics.

BERLIN

Actually, it's one lyric that isn't going as smoothly as usual.

SANDRICH

Irving, What are you talking about?
Is the script throwing you off? Don't worry.
We can always make changes.

BERLIN

The script's fine. I like the title, *Holiday Inn*.
And you got Astaire and Crosby. Good work.
But I am not so sure about your female lead, Marjorie Reynolds.

SANDRICH

Marjorie? She's great. She acts, she dances...

BERLIN

But she doesn't sing...at least not well enough.

SANDRICH

You mean not well enough for a Berlin song.

BERLIN

I've said my piece.

SANDRICH

This is not a problem. (INTO INTERCOM)
Millie! Millie.

OPENING OF DOOR

MILLIE

Yes, Mr. Sandrich.

SANDRICH

Why don't you answer the intercom?

MILLIE

It makes my voice sound funny.

SANDRICH

How can you tell?

MILLIE

When you speak on the Intercom, it sounds funny.
I don't want my voice to sound like that in here, especially when you have guests.

SANDRICH

Millie, has Martha Mears arrived yet?

MILLIE

No. She is still recording at the sound stage.
They'll be finished in a few minutes.
She knows to come here.

SHUTS DOOR

SANDRICH

Irving, you got to hear this girl.
She's a miracle. She can imitate any actress's speaking voice and turn it into a singing voice.
So, Martha will record the songs in advance and Marjorie will mouth the lyrics in front of the camera.

BERLIN

Is that legal?

SANDRICH

It's a whole new world of movie magic, Irving.
Welcome to 1941.

KNOCK ON DOOR

SANDRICH
Come in, Millie.

DOOR OPENS

MILLIE
Miss Mears is here.

SANDRICH
Then send her in.

MARTHA
I am in. Hello Mr. Sandrich.

SANDRICH
Hello Martha. I'm glad you will be lending your voice to our film.

MARTHA
Actually, I am selling my voice to your film.
But I'd be honored to sing any song by Irving Berlin, even if I had to do it as Minnie Mouse.

BERLIN
Were you recording today?

MARTHA
Actually, what I was doing was dubbing.
But yeah, today was a triple-header:
Carole Landis
(SING) "Our Memory Lane should seem much sweeter,
if I had known you all the while."

Veronica Lake:

Julio Martinez

(SING) "I long to be a lovely thing, how I'd cling,
for I was born to love."

And that starlet from Hungary, Eva Gabor:
(SING) "We met in Paris at Café Du Dome.
He was so Grand and I was so far from home.
He would change my accent from no to merci
And teach me the meaning of oui, oui cheri."

CLAPPING FROM BERLIN AND SANDRICH

BERLIN
Miss Mears, I would be honored to have you sing my songs.

MARTHA
Martha, please. So what do ya got?

SANDRICH
Mr. Berlin, your piano awaits.

SOUND OF SHEET MUSIC BEING UNFOLDED

IRVING
Can you sight read, Miss Mears?

MARTHA
Mr. Berlin, I can sight read paint splatter on a wall.
Please, call me Martha.

BERLIN STARTS PLAYING THE INTRO TO 'BE CAREFUL, IT'S MY HEART' WHILE TALKING

BERLIN (TO SANDRICH)
O.K. This is from the Valentines Day segment.

Bing sings this, while Fred hijacks Marjorie onto the dance floor.
It's meant to be purely a solo for Bing,
but I'd like to hear how it would sound with a female voice.
Maybe we'll change things up.
Let's take it from the verse Miss...
I mean Martha, if you please.

MARTHA

I do please.

(SINGING)
"Be careful, it's my heart.
It's not my watch you're holding, it's my heart.
It's not the note I sent you
That you quickly burned.
It's not the book I lent you
That you never returned.
Remember, it's my heart."

(SPEAKING) Zowee. This is beautiful.

SANDRICH

Irving, I think you've got a hit.

BERLIN

I'm counting on it.

SANDRICH

All right now. What about our big finale tune?

BERLIN

That's what I meant about things not going smoothly.
I've got the melody, but the lyrics, I've got nothing.

SANDRICH

What? Irving Berlin cannot have nothing.

Julio Martinez

MARTHA

It would be unpatriotic.

BERLIN

Mark, the finale is set at Christmas time in rural Connecticut.
I am a Russian Jew immigrant, raised on the lower east side of New York.
What do I know about Christmas in Connecticut?

SANDRICH

Irving, you're asking me?
I was born Mark Rex Goldstein, also from New York.
So, we don't have a finale for the film.

BERLIN

Actually, I have been doodling with a verse,
But I don't think it works for the film.
Martha, come do this with me.
Maybe it will inspire me.

MARTHA

You betcha.

BERLIN STARTS PLAYING

BERLIN

(SINGING)
"The sun is shining,

MARTHA

(SINGING) ...the grass is green.

BERLIN

The orange and palm trees sway.

MARTHA
There's never been such a day in Beverly Hills, LA

BERLIN
But it's December the 24th

MARTHA
And I'm longing to be up North...."
(SPEAK SINGING) Are you gong to leave me dangling up here on a dominant 7th chord?

BERLIN
I'll get back to you.

THEY ALL LAUGH

SANDRICH
Irving, I have complete faith in you.

KNOCK ON THE DOOR

SANDRICH
Come in Millie.

DOOR OPENS

MILLIE
There is an art director out here waiting to show you sketches.

BERLIN
I gotta go anyway.

MARTHA
Me too, Mr. Sandrich, unless you want me to hum a few bars of your wallpaper.

SANDRICH
Just a second, Martha.
Well, Irving, is she or isn't she?

BERLIN
Yes! Martha is our singing Marjorie.
I look forward to working with you.

MARTHA
You betcha. See you folks. (AS SHE IS WALKING AWAY)

BERLIN
Well, I'm...

SANDRICH
One minute more, Irving.
Millie, didn't you grow up in Connecticut?

MILLIE
Close. Maine.

SANDRICH
But you've been to Connecticut?

MILLIE
Well, you do have to pass through it to get to Maine.

SANDRICH
So, what is Connecticut like in December?

MILLIE
White! Very, very white.

BERLIN
White? O.K., that's more than I had before.
Let's see what I come up with.

I'LL BE HOME FOR CHRISTMAS (MHS RECORDING)

SANDRICH
Millie, where is Irving Berlin?

MILLIE
On the soundstage.

SANDRICH
What's he doing down there?

MILLIE
Oh, I don't know, maybe recording all the songs for *Holiday Inn.*

SANDRICH
What? How come I didn't know?
What idiot gave them the go ahead to start recording?

MILLIE
You. I refer to your production memo, dated, August 7, 1941.

SANDRICH
I know what year it is.

MILLIE
Good. The memo clearly states that vocal rehearsals will proceed from August 15 to August 31.
And that vocal recordings of the complete song score with full orchestra will commence on September 3. That is today.

SANDRICH
Fine! Fine! So who is down there right now?

MILLIE
Everyone who is singing is down there, including Martha Mears.

And of course, Mr. Berlin and that other composer who is doing the background score.

SANDRICH

Robert Dolan?

MILLIE

Yes him. And there is also the choreographer Danny Dare.
We have a full house.

SANDRICH

Well call down there.
I need to speak to Irving.

BERLIN

No need to tire yourself.
Millie called down, said you needed to talk.
What's up?

SANDRICH

Are you on a break?

BERLIN

Lunch. You can starve the actors, but the musicians have to eat.

SANDRICH

So, everything is moving along fine?

BERLIN

Like a pushcart on Hester Street.
You have concerns?

SANDRICH

I'm happy if you're happy.
I just have a question about the Christmas time song.

The Eight Plays of Christmas

BERLIN

You don't like it?

SANDRICH

Are you kidding?
From one Jew to another, that may be the best
Christmas song since *Silent Night*.
Irving, your lyric is a miracle.
I just have a question about the melody.

BERLIN

What about the melody? It works.

SANDRICH

Of course it works. It's perfect.
But I have the feeling, I've heard it before.
Irving, tell me, you didn't by chance borrow it from somewhere or someone?

BERLIN

Mark, you got me. Actually, I stole it...from myself.
Can you remember back to 1935, when I was working on *Top Hat* with Fred and Ginger?

SANDRICH

It does come to mind.
I directed it.

BERLIN

Right. I played that very melody for you and Fred.
Fred loved it but you said it wasn't right for the film.

SANDRICH

Yeah, yeah. I remember now.
It wasn't right for *Top Hat,*
But it could just win you an Oscar for *Holiday Inn*.
What did Bing Think?

Julio Martinez

BERLIN
Oh, when I first played it for him, Bing just kind of yawned and said, "I don't think we have any problems with that one, Irving."

INTERLUDE MUSIC

MARTHA
Hiya Millie. How's tricks?

MILLIE
I'd say hectic but that would be a gross understatement.
Location filming began on Monday, December First, but Mr. Sandrich has been up in Sonoma since November 15.
Working on location can be its own kind of hell.

MARTHA
Where are they shooting?

MILLIE
The Village Inn Resort in Monte Rio, on the Russian River.
It's the stand in for the Holiday Inn in Connecticut.

MARTHA
Sounds great. You know, someday I'd like to actually sing in front of the cameras, instead of a stuffy four feet by four feet recording booth.

MILLIE
Speaking of singing, why are you here?
You were done weeks ago.
You got another dubbing session.

MARTHA
Actually I'm back on *Holiday Inn.*
Your boss likes Mr. Berlin's opening theme, *Happy Holiday*, so much, he wants it to recur throughout the film.

The Eight Plays of Christmas

So, I'm back in my four-by-four box.
I had an hour to kill so I thought I'd hang around here.
O.K.?

MILLIE

O.K. Actually, I think you have the best job in the world.
You sing for a living and get paid well for it.
And you don't just dub other people. I've heard you on the radio.
And you've recorded with people like Hoagy Carmichael.
There was a time when I would have given anything to do that.

MARTHA

Whoa, whoa there lady. You sing?

MILLIE

Two years a vocal major at Juilliard.

MARTHA

Drop my drawers. Julliard?
What happened?

MILLIE

The Depression finally caught up with my family.
I had to quit Juilliard and get a job.
I learned to type and take dictation.
And here I am today.

MARTHA

Come with me.

MILLIE

Where?

MARTHA

Into your boss's office.
I wanna hear some undiscovered talent.

Julio Martinez

MILLIE
Martha, it's been years.

MARTHA
You went to Julliard.
You must be able to read music.

MILLIE
Well, to quote a chanteuse I know,
I can sight read paint splatter on a wall.

MARTHA
The soundman pressed me a record of the accompaniment.
Here's the lead sheet. You sing the lead and I'll do the harmony.
We'll be two thirds of the Andrews Sisters.

MARTHA PUTS THE RECORD ON THE PHONOGRAPH

MILLIE
I don't know about this.

MARTHA
Sing!
MARTHA & MILLIE SING 'HAPPY HOLIDAY'
"If you're burdened down with trouble
If your nerves are wearin' thin.
Park your load down the road
And come to Holiday Inn.
Happy holiday, happy holiday
May the calendar keep bringing
Happy holidays to you."

MARTHA
Millie! You can sing.
What are you doing sitting behind a typewriter.
I can get you vocal work. You could...

MILLIE

Martha, Martha, thank you.
Singing with you has been a real kick.
But, it is really not for me.
I like sitting behind my typewriter.
I like my job and I am very good at it.

MARTHA

Well, if Sandrich gives you a hard time, call me.
I'll squeeze you into my four by four booth.

MILLIE

Thank you. Oh, speaking of Mr. Sandrich,
I've got to contact him.
We have to find a different caterer for his evening shoots.

MARTHA

He's shooting day and night.

MILLIE

Right through Saturday, six straight days.
But he's given me strict orders not to contact him on Sunday.
He is going bar his hotel door and sleep all day.

PHONE RINGING (FOUR INTENSE RINGS)

SANDRICH

(SLEEPY) Wha? Hello? Who the hell is this?

MILLIE

Mr. Sandrich, it's Millie.

SANDRICH

Millie? Didn't you listen? This is my day off.
I don't want to be disturbed by any one, even you.
Now go away and....

MILLIE

Mr. Sandrich! The Japanese have bombed our naval fleet in Hawaii.

SANDRICH

Wha? What? Are you sure?

MILLIE

It came over the studio's AP wire 15 minutes ago.
They attacked some port I never hear of...Pearl Harbor.

SANDRICH

Oh, my God.

MILLIE

Sir! Mr. Sandrich, are we at war?

SANDRICH

Yes, I believe we are.

I'LL BE HOME FOR CHRISTMAS INTERLUDE

BERLIN

Don't get me wrong, Mark.
I am delighted to have Bing Crosby singing one of my songs on Christmas Day, over a national radio broadcast.
But are you sure you want to give this song away before the film is even completed and distributed.

SANDRICH

Irving, This is the perfect day and time for Bing to introduce it.

MILLIE

It's time. I'm turning on the radio.

KEN CARPENTER
(ORCHESTRAL INTRO UNDERCORING THE ANNOUNCER)
Welcome to this Christmas day, 1941 broadcast of Kraft Music Hall starring Bing Crosby, with Mary Martin, Jack Carson, John Scott Trotter and his Orchestra, the Music Maids and Hal Hopper. To begin our show, Bing is going to introduce a new song by Irving Berlin that is soon to be featured in Paramount Pictures' upcoming film musical, *Holiday Inn*, starring Bing Crosby, Fred Astaire and Marjorie Reynolds.

Bing would like to perform it now as a special Christmas Day gift to the men and women in uniform who may be far away from home during Christmastime next year.

Accompanied by John Scott Trotter, his orchestra and chorus, ladies and gentlemen, Bing Crosby.

BING CROSBY ('WHITE CHRISTMAS' RECORDING)

SOUND OF RADIO BENG TURNED OFF

MILLIE
You're turning off Bing Crosby?

SANDRICH
I heard what I wanted to hear.
Irving, you really did it.

BERLIN
You know Mark, when I first showed the song to my wife, Ellin, she looked at it and said, "Irvie, there are only 54 words in this song. Did you run out of ideas?"
I just felt the song said everything it needed to say.

SANDRICH
I agree. And Bing Crosby really sold it.

MILLIE
Actually, Mr. Sandrich and Mr, Berlin, I believe *White Christmas* is going to be very popular for a very long time, no matter who is singing it.

THE DRIFTERS VERSION OF 'WHITE CHRISTMAS,' UNDERSCORING THE READING OF THE CREDITS BY THR ACTOR PLAYING KEN CARPENTER

KEN CARPENTER
On a historical note. The Irving Berlin song, *White Christmas*, went on to win the 1943 Academy Award for Best original Song and established itself as the most played and requested Christmas song during World War II.

Today, according to *Guinness Book of World Records*, Bing Crosby's version is the best selling single of all time, with sales in excess of 50 million.

Largely due to the immense popularity of the song, *White Christmas*, director/producer Mark Sandrich decided to make a follow-up to *Holiday Inn*, called *Blue Skies,* starring Bing Crosby and Fred Astaire, featuring a score by Irving Berlin.

In 1945, while in pre-production, Sandrich died suddenly of heart failure at age 44.

At his memorial service, Sandrich's wife affirmed that her husband had felt his highest career achievement to date, was producing the film that led to the creation of *White Christmas.*

The End

Printed in Great Britain
by Amazon